THE LAUNDRY LIST

All the Things I Forgot to Tell You about Laundry and Life

Lisa James McKenzie

Illustrated by Keesha Freskiw

ISBN: 978-0-9947-4520-0 (sc)

Library of Congress Control Number: 2015917161

Because of the dynamic nature of the Internet, any web addresses or links contained in this book may have changed since publication and may no longer be valid.

Published by Warrior Girl Press

Printed by Lulu Publishing Services
rev. date: 1/7/2016

CONTENTS

• •

For Lindsay,

I wrote this book in honour of your graduation from high school and launching an independent life at university. I'm so proud of you, so proud to have a daughter who is such a bright light: smart, thoughtful, funny, loving, kind and brave. You are strong in ways I am not. Dare I say you are a little like your father? In all the best ways.

I'll always be there if you need me, whether by phone, text, email or carrier pigeon. All you have to do is send the message, and I'll send one right back. *On my way.* Always. It doesn't matter where you are.

Be big and tall, my beloved angel of love and light.

Love,
Mom

Don't believe what I say. Decide for yourself what is true.
—Siddhartha Gautama (the Buddha),
an extremely loose translation

PREFACE

A Mixed Bag, Deliberate and Inspired

Dear Daughter,

Let me explain what you hold in your hands. It is not exactly a laundry manual, though there are tips and instructions sprinkled here and there throughout its pages. I may do a lot of laundry, but I'm no expert, so I would be remiss to hold myself out as one. Nor is it purely a book of essays inspired by my experiences in the laundry room, though there are a few of those too. The truth is, in all my years washing clothes, not much has really happened in the laundry room, at least not in terms of high-tension drama or explosive events. (Though there was that one time Dad tried to poison me, inadvertently, by mixing bleach and ammonia. "Cleaning solution o' death," your sister Sarah called it. Then again, that was really a *cleaning* incident, not a *laundry* incident, even though he found the ingredients in the cupboard above the laundry tub.)

This is a book of lessons in laundry and in life, expressed in a variety of ways.

Lesson 1: It's a bad idea to mix household chemicals.

This book is a mixed bag: incident reports from the front lines of the laundry room, instructional memos, advice from neighbours, bullet-pointed checklists and yes, the occasional story. There's even a recipe for dippy eggs (because Gramper insisted). Taken together, there is no unity of style in this book whatsoever, and as I understand it, that isn't how books are supposed to be written, in this sprawling, all-over-the-place, a-little-of-this-and-a-dash-of-that fashion.

But that's how this book asked to be written. And who am I to argue?

What you won't find here is anything that purely "belongs" in a book about laundry, such as an exhaustive list of stain removal tricks (if such a thing is even possible). That's not the point, and others have done that job far better than I ever will. Besides, I know you will conduct independent research and create your own solutions from healthy, environmentally friendly ingredients that won't make you sneeze or break out in hives.

What the pieces do have in common are laundry, life lessons and inspired beginnings. There had to be a scrap of wisdom (or humour) worth taking beyond the boundaries of the laundry room. (And I'm sorry, but no, I couldn't find that flicker of life in a description of how to best wash an alpaca-hair sweater; maybe I didn't look hard enough.) So if this book seems erratic, winding and tangential in its path, know that this is deliberate. And inspired.

And while we're on the subject of deliberate and inspired …

Consider for a moment how this same strategy might apply to loads of laundry, *your* loads of laundry, the ones you'll be doing at university.

Imagine yourself standing in your underwear in your dorm room one fine Sunday morning. You would really like to pull on your black yoga pants, the comfy, non-pilling, not-Lululemon ones. Unfortunately, they're wadded up in a linty ball beside your laundry basket (but with any luck, they will be free of grey cat hair, unlike the situation at home). So you have a choice: you can pick up the yoga pants and spot-wipe them with a damp facecloth or you can do the laundry. In theory, you could also choose another pair of pants from your wardrobe, but in all probability, all your comfortable lounging-about pants are either in or near the laundry basket in a similar unlaundered state. After all, you've had a busy week dashing from classes to labs to the library to the cheer gym. You've been studying, working out, training and eating healthy, and with any luck, you've squeezed in some time with friends. Laundry? Not so much. And alas, neither your mom nor the laundry fairies will be descending any time soon to sweep away the not-so-clean clothes and restore them to your closet, freshly laundered and reasonably wrinkle-free.

So you determine that yes, you will do the laundry. And this won't be the first time: In April 2011 you sent me an urgent text when I was away in Florida with Juney and Gramper: "Mom, Mom, I did the laundry!"

I always knew you could.

In any case, you fortify yourself with a strong cup of peppermint tea, unsweetened, and a cappuccino bar from Mariposa Market (received via courier from your mother, who maybe can't wash your clothes but can still feed you). Then, straightening your shoulders, you gather stray socks from the floor and the bath towel hanging over the closet door, and you toss them into the basket with the clothes. In a fit of boldness, you decide to wash the bedding too, and you yank the pillowcases and sheets off your single bed and drop the lot into the now-overflowing (albeit one-person) laundry basket. You grab the environmentally friendly, fragrance-free, gluten-free detergent on the way out the door and march confidently in the direction of the coin-op laundry room located on the bottom floor of your residence.

When you arrive, you deposit your basket on the floor beside a long row of washing machines. You now face the array of items to be laundered: three pairs of Lycra gym shorts (black, white and multicoloured), two pairs of jeans, two blouses of indeterminate fabric (one of which has a lace inset), five T-shirts (two white, three coloured), bras, socks, underwear, one organic bath towel, two facecloths and your once-white bed linens. You flip open the lid of the washer and consider the magnitude of the tub. You eye the contents of the basket again, mentally sorting into lights and darks, delicates and heavier items and calculating the number of loads it will take to properly wash everything. *Two? Three? Four? For Pete's sake*, you think, *I have cheer practice in two hours and a chemistry lab to write up. I can't be running back and forth between the machines and my books all morning.*

You weigh your options briefly; then you press your lips together, reach for the water temperature dial and set it to cold. You kneel down beside your basket, pick out the delicates and put them into mesh bags, which you then toss expertly into the open washer. With the knowing hand of a veteran, you set the wash cycle, add a half capful of detergent, pick up the basket and dump the lot into the washer, hand-fluffing everything up a bit to spread out the load.

No, Mom! I won't put jeans and whites together!

Oh yes, you might. Under the right conditions, you just might. And that's okay. Spare the load any freshly tie-dyed red-and-orange T-shirts. Leave out any brand-new blue jeans whose indigo might rub off, and everything will turn out just fine. Most of the time, pretty good is good enough.

The laundry gurus would say that, for optimum results, you should not put these items together in one load. Disaster may ensue. And I can't really dispute that, not on the basis of good laundering practices, a chosen few of which I will share in this slim volume. *Knowledge is power, and knowing when to dispense with knowledge is also power.* Sometimes you have a higher cause to attend to— something more important to do than perfect loads of laundry.

So if that is the case, why did I write you a book filled with all kinds of laundry advice, much of which I don't even follow myself? Because I don't want you to mistakenly assume that the way I do laundry is the right way. Or the only way. I do my best, but much of the time I'm just winging it, and I don't want to send you off in the world with a half-baked laundry education.

Come to think of it, that applies to just about everything I do at home.

In the laundry room and in life, it is helpful, even crucial, to know the basic rules and operating principles. We can avoid ruinous mistakes and, when the situation calls for it, reach for a higher standard. But the rules-are-rules approach can be a trap. Only you can take in the larger context: there is no substitute for your own intuition, independent judgment and an artful tossing of the rules out the laundry room window.

And with that bit of perspective tucked into your laundry basket, let us now stick our hands into this ragtag laundry hamper of a book and see what we come out with. *Delicates, anyone?*

Approximately 150 loads of laundry were washed, dried and hung in the course of writing of this book.

ACKNOWLEDGMENTS

I have always loved reading acknowledgments pages, so I am delighted to be able to write my own.

First and above all, thanks to my younger daughter, Sarah McKenzie, an outstanding writer, a voracious reader and an honest, keen-eyed editor. Sarah is always willing to read any pages I thrust in her direction. I love you!

Thank you to my mentor, editor and long-distance friend, Gloria Kempton, who has taught me much about writing and life and has also shown me that the Internet can indeed ground a great friendship. Thanks to my writing group, Tiffany, Suzanne and Sandy, as well as writing friends past, especially Antoinette, Jeni and Jamie (my first writing friends ever), Corliss, Jennifer, Susan, Valerie and so many others. Thanks to writing coach Marlee LeDai, who said, "You gotta go pro, Lisa," and to Amanda Castleman, who taught me to keep paddling when inspiration evaporated into thin (or fat) air.

Thanks to friends, extended family and neighbours who offered helpful laundry suggestions as well as support via e-mail—"Lisa, how's the book going?"—and to my inspired book club friends Sue, Janie, Laury, Dianne and Barb, who give me a safe place to share thoughts, experience, tea and great books.

To my parents, Merv and June James (a.k.a. Juney and Gramper), for their diligent copyediting and for offering enthusiastic encouragement. About everything. Pretty much always.

And thanks to my husband, Bill McKenzie, because he is the durable denim to my hand-wash cold.

INTRODUCTION

Why the Laundry Room?

Why not the kitchen?

You might think the kitchen a more logical place to focus a book intended to launch you, my beautiful daughter, into the world. Why not a volume of meal-inspired essays with recipes for tea biscuits and the good beef tucked in between? The kitchen, after all, is the place of nourishment, of Saturday morning French toast and your sister's made-with-love, gluten-free key lime pie, of soothing herbal tea (and yes, *agitating* black coffee). It's the first place you always stopped on your way into the house after school, dropping your bag on the floor and leaning on the counter to check your phone before scuttling up to your bedroom to change out of your uniform. You wouldn't zip into the laundry room when you arrived home; you'd rush right past it—unless, of course, you'd suffered a chai tea spill, and even then, it would be a quick stop to drop the offended clothing into a pail of water.

So why the laundry room?

There are many reasons.

First, in your freshman year at university, you'll have a Meal Plan, but you won't have a Laundry Plan. So you'll likely be spending time more time washing clothes than cooking. Theoretically, you could send your laundry out to be done by a service, but that would be both bad form and unduly expensive. Also, it is better to understand how to do something before delegating it to someone else.

Second, I would be remiss not to provide you with some basic laundry instructions. I believe this was a stipulation in the Unwritten Parenting Manual that arrived with you on May 6, 1996 (at precisely 8:35 a.m.). I have given you a *few* basic guidelines over the years, some of which appeared in my 2009 one-page memo, "Basic Laundry Instructions by Mom," featuring washing machine clip art and conveniently hung over the dryer. So this laundry guide business isn't unprecedented. This book is the unabridged version of "Laundry Instructions" and, as it turns out, a correction. Some of my previous advice was—I've since learned—wrong.

Now don't misunderstand me. It is not as though you are a complete novice where laundry is concerned, and it's not as though you aren't a sharp enough cookie to figure out how to do it yourself. When you were 14 you created your own list of key laundry rules, organizing them according to your own logic and carefully writing them down and adding them to the collection of Important Laundry Instructions. You prepared that list in contemplation of my being away on holiday with Juney and Gramper, and when you accomplished your first load you sent that fateful text I mentioned earlier: "Mom, Mom, I did the laundry!" Your excitement travelled 1500 miles south and onto the screen of my cell phone. I was sitting with Aunt Karen at the dining room table at the time, a smile spreading across my face as I read.

"What's up?" Aunt Karen asked.

"Lindsay did the laundry," I answered and then read the text out loud to her, and to Juney and Gramper, who were standing in the kitchen.

We laughed and nodded and smiled: *Lindsay is a James after all!*

In any case, I intend to fill in a few key laundry pointers that I may have missed over the years so that when you arrive in the coin-op Laundromat at university, you have a handy place to find maternal instruction (you know, in the unlikely event that I'm not immediately available by cell phone. *Stain? On my way!*).

Think of it as the *Pocket Mom: Laundry Room Edition.*

There are other reasons for choosing the laundry room. For me, the laundry room is a sacred place—it's *quiet*, for one thing— notwithstanding that it might look a bit chaotic at first glance: horse blankets stacked on the floor, random piles of laundry in various stages of cleanliness and a whole lot of renegade dryer lint affixed to the baseboards.

I know what you're thinking: *Sacred? Oh boy, here goes Mom getting her guru on.*

Yup, Mom, the Divine Guru of Sacred Laundry.

Bear with me, dear. As much as I don't believe in lectures and gratuitous advice, well, perhaps I just like to disguise it well.

In our house, this sacred place is a small room tucked off the back hall, its one window obstructed, more often than not, by a freshly laundered and hanging shirt. I often think of that shirt as part of our security system. Any would-be robber seeing it might think, *Hey, there's fresh laundry hanging in that house; someone must be home* … and with that small gesture, I am setting up a sort of scarecrow against thieves. So there is not just love in that laundry but personal security too!

Our laundry room is a place of meditative work and warmth, of love quietly expressed, where I escape the noise of the office to take care of you, Sarah and Dad one sock at a time, from carefully dryer-fluffed shirts to hand-washed cheerleading uniforms to horse-riding clothes carefully separated out so as to minimize aggravating your allergies (well, to the extent one can in a house with two cats). The laundry room is a refuge too, a place of solitude in a world that is sometimes too loud. Something noisy going on in the dorm? Need some peace and quiet? No problem. Run to the laundry room and turn on the washer and dryer. Run the taps if necessary. Trust me: you won't hear a thing.

And for those of us whose minds are so often engaged in arduous mental tasks, the physical work of laundry can give our brains a break. My American colleague Jan captured this perfectly in one of our rambling email exchanges.

"It is precisely that kind of activity that allows me to write," she wrote, "because it involves no contemplation of muddy gray legal problems, just tasks that need to get done (like loads of laundry). It frees up the mind for creativity."

I couldn't agree more. I've had some of my very best ideas arrive in the course of moving a load of whites from the laundry to the dryer. Maybe you will find it to be a respite too as you step into the world of health sciences (nutrition and nutraceutical sciences, to be exact).

Laundry can help you develop qualities like tenaciousness, attention to detail, patience and organization: treating and re-treating stains; separating whites from darks, heavier pieces from delicates; checking pockets for tissues before committing a pair of pants to the load and having a sense of humour when you've forgotten. The laundry room represents—more than any other room in the house—the endless, overlapping, repetitive cycles of life. Wash, dry, fold and hang; restore to closets and drawers; repeat. You can be sure that, even as you are washing one load, another pile has already started, and so laundry represents continuity, like the generations of a family.

So why not the kitchen? Doesn't a homemade, gluten-free tuna-chickpea salad or a freshly emptied dishwasher represent a lot of same things? Isn't it a place of warmth and love too?

Sure.

But for me, there is something special about the laundry room. It's a place that says, "You matter to me. And I want to make your way through the world a little easier by making sure you can find that white T-shirt when you need it." Then I will hang that shirt in your closet and quietly close your bedroom door.

So there you have it. Why the laundry? For all these reasons and this: it's always going to be there. Just like me.

Bring laundry home every month for your mom to wash.
—Aaron Moore, cousin and PhD.

Chapter 1

FIRST PRINCIPLES

A Few Ideas to Smooth the Wrinkles on Your Laundry Path

Laundry is one of those things in life that, done well, can be a great comfort, a foundation thread that helps hold everything together. Done poorly or not at all, it can be a persistent source of irritation. There's a lot to be said for a crisp white shirt hanging in your closet, clean and ready to wear when you need it, or fresh sheets welcoming you into bed at night, especially if they were hung to dry in a summer breeze. Okay, I've never hung sheets to dry in a summer breeze, but we can dream, can we not?

With that in mind, here's a quick list of basic principles for you to consider as you set out on your own laundry path:

1. **Keep the end in mind.** Your mission, should you choose to accept it, is to keep your clothing, towels and bed linens in good condition and to neatly restore them to their respective closets or drawers once laundered. Perhaps that sounds

obvious, but keep in mind that laundry starts long before you open the lid of the washing machine.

2. **Embrace reasonable standards.** When I was a teenager, I had a friend whose European mom ironed all her T-shirts and, allegedly, all her father's underwear. Now, it is not for me to judge someone else's laundry or lifestyle choices, but for my part, I can think of happier, more productive ways to spend my time than ironing an article of clothing that will become wrinkled within 15 minutes of my pulling it over my head. Find a reasonable middle ground. (Of course, if ironing is your meditation, then that is something else entirely.)

3. **Don't create more work for yourself than necessary.** Dropping your just-worn clothes on the floor as you undress may seem like a quick-and-easy approach to laundry management, but is it really? No. It's a deferred decision to that all important question—will I wear those pants again, or do they need to be washed?—and the longer you leave them on the floor, the more linty, crumply and unwearable they will become. So take a moment to put things where they belong—either in the laundry basket, back on the hanger or in a drawer—and spare yourself more work later.

4. **An ounce of prevention is worth a pound of stain remover.** One day as Sarah and I drove along Highway 12, she caught sight of a car in her rear-view mirror that was following us much too closely. "In Driver's Ed, they teach us that car accidents don't just happen," she said, lightly touching the

brakes to back off the tailgater. "They develop." The same is true for stains, so take a few precautionary measures: wear an apron when you're cooking, especially if tomatoes or red wine are involved. If you need to check the oil in your car, don't do it while wearing your favourite blouse. Designate old clothes for garden work, painting and other clothing-hazardous jobs.

5. **Time is not on your side where stains are concerned, so act accordingly.** The longer that tea stain steeps into the hem of your white peasant blouse, the tougher it will be to remove later. Stains happen. Deal with them. Double-quick.

6. **Check the care label.** Care labels are to clothes what the owner's manual is to your car. Okay, perhaps your car is a little more complicated, but both have basic maintenance guidelines, and paying attention to them is a great starting point if you want your clothes and linens to last. Care labels can help you avoid ruining a favourite shirt or fading your bright pink towels, not to mention saving you time and money in buying replacements.

7. **Embrace the right tools for the job.** This follows from rule 6. That includes choice of detergent, water temperature, drying method and so on.

8. **When in doubt, hand wash cold.** If you love that delicate white-lace blouse, then treat it with the gentlest washing method available: the *manual* one. Don't take unnecessary risks with things that are precious to you.

9. **Embrace regular maintenance of your laundry equipment.** Obviously if you are using a coin-op laundry, it isn't *your*

equipment per se, but you should still get into the habit of cleaning the lint filter on the dryer and understand that the machines themselves need to be looked after if they are going to serve you well. This rule applies to a lot of things in life, like spouses, cars, friendships and houses. (See the chapter called "A Rat's Nest in the Dryer Vent" for more on maintenance.)

10. **Be kind to the environment.** Use the hot-water cycle and the dryer thoughtfully: both consume electricity at a voracious rate. You don't need to reach for harsh chemicals or fancy products to manage stains either. Lemon juice and vinegar work wonders on sweat stains, baking soda boosts washing power and hydrogen peroxide can make ballpoint pen stains vanish.

11. **Forgive yourself; you're not a machine.** I created this tip list in a Kitchener hotel room while you and I spent three days at the Cheerleading Provincials. When we arrived home late on a Sunday night, I unpacked our bags on the floor of the laundry room and cracked open the lid of the washing machine lid to start a fresh load. What did I find? A bunch of towels half-dried and spun-plastered to the sides of the washer. I sighed, closed the lid and then noticed the little shadowbox on the wall above the machine. It was a gift from Aunt Pego, a miniature washing machine and the motto "What if success is getting the clothes from the washer to the dryer before mildew sets in?" We do our best, and some days our best is kind of stinky. That's okay. There's always the next load.

Sheets and towels do not need to happen weekly. This is something our mothers came up with, God bless them. Once every two weeks is good enough.
—Karen Secord-Hamilton, neighbour

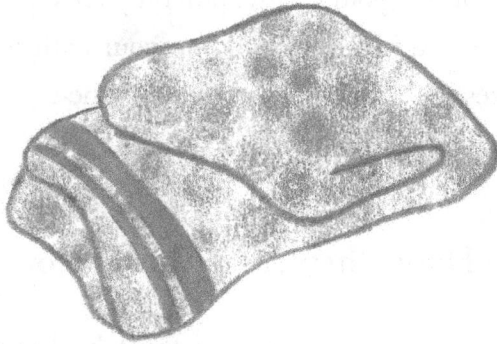

Chapter 2

BATHROOM TOWEL PRACTICES

To Hang or Not to Hang Is Not Even a Question[1]

You might think a book about laundry would confine its advice to the laundry room. But no. Good laundry practices begin the moment you unbutton your blouse, pull off your socks or decide how (or, heaven forbid, *whether*) to hang up your bath towel. How you handle the threshold from clean to dirty is the critical first step in an effective laundering system. So let's talk towels!

You Need to Hang Them, and This Is How

Towels that are damp from use must be hung up. Most of the time, in our house, this rule of bath towel etiquette has been observed. If we're in a hurry, though, we might be tempted to drop our still-wet towels on the floor, possibly in close proximity to or *on top of* cheer shoes, school supplies or unwitting cats. This will result in mildewing remedied only by an immediate trip to the

---

[1] And if you think it's a question, then you'd better keep white vinegar in stock. You'll be using a lot of it to get rid of the mildew smell.

washing machine (sparing the felines, of course). If the towels and any underlying clothing get really stinky, you might need to wash them with vinegar. Repeatedly. If you want to generate a lot of unnecessary work for yourself, this is a good way to go about it.

Let's start by making sure we always hang up towels. And while we're on the subject, in order to fully and properly *dry*, towels need to be unscrunched and separated from one another. Do not hang wet towels folded in half, in a clump or on top of other wet towels, or you will end up with a less-than-fresh-smelling pile and another unwarranted trip to the washing machine.

How Many to Use and Where to Hang Them

I don't know how this happened exactly, but our family has developed a habit of using the entire bathroom towel collection all at once and all the time. For each shower or bath, two bath towels are engaged (one for drying the body and one for hair, except in Dad's case for obvious—or shall we say *bald*—reasons). Said towels are then draped over the hall banisters, where they remain, often for days, while fresh towels are pulled from the bathroom linen supply for each subsequent bath or shower. At some point, the entire bathroom linen closet may stand empty, while the upstairs banisters are lined with a dozen towels in varying stages of wetness. Guests entering our home's gracious front foyer with its vaulted ceiling and curving staircase are greeted with a veritable flag display of bathroom towels. No need for fancy sculpture or artwork here: *welcome to our home, ladies and gentlemen, where we take a* lot *of showers, and we're not afraid to show it.*

This bold display of towel use contrasts sharply with the bathroom linen methods embraced in my childhood home, where precisely two bath towels, one hand towel and one washcloth would be deployed at a time. Towels and washcloths not in use remained firmly folded and stationed in the closet, clean and untouched, awaiting their own independent tour of duty. Items in service were not permitted to depart their assigned space but would instead be hung carefully on the towel racks *in the bathroom,* post-shower. Any person allowing bathroom linens to go AWOL into the more public spaces of the home would face severe reprimands (such as maternal lip pursing).

What do these differing methods of bathroom towel use have to do with laundry, you ask?

From a laundering point of view, there is a decided disadvantage to the all-at-once method. First of all, it's hard to keep track of which towels need laundering, since they are all mashed together. Second, there is the endless chore of folding up the banistered towels, once they are suitably dry, and then stacking them on the floor pending further decision. And let us ask, Can we put used-but-dry towels back in the linen closet? Wait a minute: Should we be folding them at all? Surely bath towels have accumulated body oils, at a minimum, or a makeup stain or two, and folding them up seems, well, as my four-year-old-self once said, *unsanitary.*

And if you can gird yourself against that reality, do you just leave the used towels in stacks of three right there on the hall floor? Or do you move them 10 paces northwest to a spot just outside the bathroom door? What happens if you are in the shower and need a towel or two? Catastrophe. You have to either call out to your sister for help, or tiptoe out of the shower and across the tile floor, hoping the shower curtain rod won't be displaced in the process, thwacking you on the head. It's just better to have a few fresh, reasonably clean towels awaiting on the hooks installed outside the bathtub. Wouldn't you agree?

From proper towel etiquette we will move on to clothes, but first let's hear it for facecloths.

**What if success is just getting the wash into
the dryer before mildew sets in?
—Aunt Pego**

Chapter 3

FACECLOTHS AND BREAD BAGS

A Lesson in Economy of Use

Did you ever stop to consider the impact of a single facecloth?

No? Me neither. At least, not until I went on vacation with Juney, Gramper and Aunt Karen.

It happened like this. We were all in Florida together, a rare treat. I can't remember *ever* being on a vacation with Aunt Karen, not even when we were kids, let alone at the advanced ages of 42 and 51. Aunt Karen and I were sitting at the dining room table, post-breakfast, half-finished coffee cups between us. We were fixed on our laptop screens checking in with business and domestic crises at home. Then Gramper came downstairs, still in his pyjamas, with a beard of white shaving cream. He looked like Santa Claus but for his still-dark hair.

"Where's mom?" he asked. "In the laundry room?"

Aunt Karen and I nodded. Gramper walked through the kitchen, opened the garage door and peered out to where Juney was standing at the washing machine.

"Juney, is there a facecloth out there, or do you want me to get a new one?"

Aunt Karen and I looked at each other.

Gramper trundled out to the garage. There was a low exchange of words between him and Juney, and though we strained to listen, we couldn't hear what was said. Gramper returned, no facecloth in hand, and made his way back up the stairs. The door of the linen closet squeaked open, closed again. Then we heard the bathroom tap turn on.

What just happened?

Gramper came all the way downstairs, midway through his morning ablutions, to ask if there was a less-than-fresh facecloth he should be using. He could have just grabbed a clean one from the closet beside the bathroom, but he didn't. The transaction cost of that decision was—what—five minutes? Isn't that unusual behaviour in our drive-thru, disposable, I-need-it-now world? Wouldn't most of us just grab a fresh one without a second thought?

I think so.

This frugality-of-use mindset is what I grew up with. It informed a lot of what went on in my childhood home, not to mention what got pinned to the clothesline. For instance, when I was a kid, plastic bags would be hand-washed in warm soapy water, rinsed thoroughly and hung to dry on a clothesline stretching from the house to a hydro pole in the backyard: long, skinny Wonder bread bags with their trade-mark red, blue and yellow dots; hot dog and hamburger bags; red-striped Vim skim-milk powder bags. This was back in the days when plastic sacks weren't multiplying exponentially as they are now, before green recycling bins appeared in every garage. Plastic bags weren't thrown out, and fresh facecloths weren't used with reckless abandon.

Juney and Gramper didn't toss stuff absentmindedly into the laundry hamper either. Towels and facecloths had a once-per-week laundry cycle and they still do, according to Juney. Clothes weren't relegated to the hamper immediately after wearing unless they were undies or obviously sweaty or soiled. These are ideas worth examining, don't you think? What Gramper did out of habit? Pausing before grabbing something fresh? Plastic bags washed and reused. In this world, where everything is so abundant, so easy, it's worth taking the sacred pause to weigh a certain frugality against less thoughtful use.

With that in mind, here are suggested guidelines for when to wash what (bread bags not included):

Bedding and Bathroom Towels

Here are some alternatives for you to consider:

- Once per week, unless someone is sick (Juney's rule)
- Every two weeks (as practised by Karen Secord-Hamilton, our one-time neighbour)
- Whenever it occurs to me—my personal preference, subject always to smell-testing for mildew and visual review for obvious stains

Clothing

Like facecloths, many clothing items may be used more than once before being relegated to the laundry pile. Here are when-to-wash guidelines organized by item:

- Underwear: one wear
- Swimsuits: one wear. Salt and chlorinated water take a toll, so *at a minimum*, rinse well after wearing.
- Sportswear (as in "worn to play sports"): one wear
- Socks, stockings and tights: one wear
- Bras: three to four wears
- T-shirts, camisoles and tank tops: one wear
- Blouses and dresses: one to three wears; the closer-fitting, the sooner you'll launder.
- Leggings and dress pants: two to four wears
- Jeans: four to five wears
- Shorts: one to five wears. The shorter they are, the more quickly they wrinkle at the hip and the more tenacious those wrinkles are.
- Skirts: one to five wears. The slimmer the fit, the more often you'll have to wash a skirt because wrinkles set in faster and with greater determination (after one to two wears). Looser, flowing skirt cuts require less care (four to five wears).
- Outer top layers (jackets, sweaters): How often these need laundering depends on what you're wearing *under* them. If you wear only a camisole, the outer layer will get stinky

faster. If you have a layer of fabric between your underarm and the garment, you may get several wears. Keep an eye on cuffs and collar, as these spots soil more quickly than the rest of the garment.

- PJs: three to four wears, perhaps less in hot weather!

Bonus Bread-Bag Clip Tip

Admittedly, this bit of advice has nothing to do with laundry but everything to do with economy and personal security. Juney didn't just recycle bread bags. She also kept the little plastic clips used to keep those bags closed. I keep them too. I don't know why, since I've never figured out what to do with them, apart from using them as a makeshift weapon, the sort of thing I'd use to fend off my older brother, Dave, who would occasionally rat-tail me with a tea towel while we were washing the dishes.

Here's how to flick a bread-bag clip:

- Break the clip in half.
- Affix the clip to the tip of your middle finger, tucking the sharp curved part of the clip just under your fingernail. The clip will now be standing up on the tip of your finger, ready for action.
- Bend your loaded finger back toward your palm and press you thumb against the middle of it as a temporary lock.
- Aim clip-loaded fingertip at intended target, being careful to avoid the face.

- Press middle finger hard into your thumb to create tension, then release, allowing middle finger to fly forward, launching clip from fingertip toward target.
- Run like heck.

CARE LABELS: A MODEST PROPOSAL

Avoid Cats *Mandatory for black yoga pants*	**Size Instability Caution** *Shrinkage may occur*	**Do Not Sleep In** *It will get stretched right out of shape*
Girlfriend friendly *To be affixed to boyfriend's clothes*	**Avoid Rain** *Becomes Sheer When Wet*	**Do Not Lend** *You may never see it again*
Mandatory matching *To address orphan-risk*	**Stain Alert** *Do not wear while eating tomato sauce*	**Hanger caution** *Mind the shoulders*

Chapter 4

BEFORE YOU CROSS THE THRESHOLD TO THE LAUNDRY ROOM

Laundry Pile Management Techniques

The Space between the Hamper and the Closet

In the "First Principles" chapter, I suggested you could spare yourself extra work by not dropping your worn-but-still-reasonably-fresh clothes on the floor. So if clothes aren't quite ready for the laundry pile, what do you do with them? Here are a few stay-fresh ideas!

- Shake items out with a few firm wrist-snaps before refolding or hanging. This will oust any loose surface soil or lint and discourage wrinkles. It's also good training should you ever find yourself facing an angry bull with only a tea towel in hand.
- Items that are especially wrinkled can be given a quick spray with water (or homemade wrinkle-releaser; see below) before hanging them up.

- It's preferable, if space allows, to place gently worn items where they benefit from airing out as opposed to putting them back in the closet or drawer. I have a whole chair in my bedroom dedicated to this purpose. Come to think of it, perhaps we should patent that? *The Dedicated Laundry Chair!*
- If your jeans have gotten baggy about the knees, toss them in the dryer for a few minutes. They'll return to their usual shape in no time.

Homemade Wrinkle Releaser

- 1/2 cup of water
- 1 generous teaspoonful of fabric softener, or
- a combination of water, essential oil and white vinegar in place of fabric softener, but then you have to contend with smelling like flowers and vinegar.
- spray bottle with a mist setting

Combine ingredients in the spray bottle, and shake with authority (the bottle, not yourself). Spray the item lightly. We don't want it soaking wet. Gently stretch and smooth the fabric to encourage wrinkles to release. The item will now be damp and may need half an hour or more to dry. If you are impatient, though, you can always wear it and use your own body as a warming rack to dry it more quickly.

If clothes have passed the point of *no return to the closet*, then it's time to hit the hamper. Here are a few thoughts on managing your dirty laundry.

Use a hamper.

Some folks deposit their dirty clothes on the floor precisely in the spot where they have gotten undressed, thereby leaving an obstacle course of laundry molehills from one end of the bedroom to the other. This method—or lack thereof—can wreak havoc on vacuuming routines as well as safety in traversing the bedroom floor (especially if you are making a nocturnal trip to the bathroom and your unsuspecting feet become entangled in a pair of twisted-up long underwear). Neatening routines in support of efficient vacuuming are, of course, subject matter for a whole other book. Accordingly, use a hamper to rustle up items for the laundry.

Turn clothes right-side-out before they hit the hamper.

The way you throw the clothes into the hamper *matters*. If you have to peel your slim-cut jeans off your body and, in the process, they turn themselves inside-out, then at some point, before you can wear them again, you'll have to turn them right-side-out. This may sound trivial, but when you have a dozen pairs of socks, two long-sleeved shirts and three sets of slim-leg pants coming out of the washing machine inside-out, load after load after load, believe me, you'll begin to notice how long it takes to right them. You might start to feel a wee bit prickly about it. So spare yourself the late-game irritation and straighten out your clothes before they are anywhere near the laundry room.

This rules applies for tights, leggings, sweatshirts, socks and, well, just about everything.[2]

---

[2] Exception: If you want to protect the exterior of clothing with a delicate design, or if you have a garment where the dye may rub off on other items, washing it inside out may be a wise course of action. More on that later. For now, just understand that for every hard-and-fast rule in laundry, as in life, there is an equally hard-and-fast exception. Contradiction is the nature of our human existence. Just embrace it, and things will go more smoothly.

The Laundry Room
A Place to Sort out Life One Load at a Time

Chapter 5

SORTING, LOADING AND MURPHY'S LAW OF TISSUE

Where We Get down to Business

Welcome to the laundry room! *Finally,* you must be thinking. Before we heave the first load into the washing machine, though, let's talk about a few preliminaries that will help you avoid inadvertent colour transfer, fabric damage and the wandering washing machine.

The Laws of Sorting

I read an expert's article about proper laundry sorting methods and was startled by the following rather complex laundry pile categorization suggested by the author:

- washing method: regular, permanent press, gentle machine-washing, hand washing
- color: white, off-white, mostly white, pastel colours, bright colours, darks and outright black

- level of soiling: where we consider type and degree of soil
- potential to inflict damage: as in hooks, zippers, large buttons
- potential to suffer damage: as in delicate fabrics prone to linting, snagging and tearing, as well as delicate details like sequins, beading and ribbon
- potential for disbursing lint: such as fluffy, new towels
- potential for picking up lint: such as pill-prone yoga pants

If you follow this methodology, you will end up with about 25 small piles of items, scattered like so many molehills on the laundry-room floor. You couldn't actually make this many piles in a standard laundry room. They would leak out the door and escape into the hall, and you would then spend the rest of your days doing loads of one-to-three items at a time. You can just imagine what happens when the same categorization is applied to the dryer. Heck, why bother with a dryer? Why not just hold those jeans up in the air and blow on them?

You get the picture. These are all wise considerations but completely unworkable unless you are doing laundry for the entire university football team. (And *no*, I don't suggest you do that. Have you ever experienced the stench of men's sports equipment? Dare I say gas mask?) So what's the answer to these piles? Compromise, and in doing so, use the laundering method associated with the items most likely to suffer damage. Use mesh bags. Turn problematic items inside out. If you're worried about a particular item, hand wash it individually.

The Allergy Exception

Mind the allergies: in our house, horse-riding clothes get their own load, colour be damned, lest we instigate a fit of repetitive sneezing.

A Word about Pilling

Any number of people I spoke to about laundry tried to correct my use of the word "pill."

"Don't you mean pull?" a few asked.

I would sigh and think, *Ah, the poor plebes.*

"No, I do not mean pull, I mean *pill*, which means to become rough with or mat into little balls, as defined by the Oxford dictionary."

If they happened to be wearing a wool sweater at the time, I would search their sleeves for an example.

"And if you must know, it is derived from the Middle English *pylle*, from Anglo-French *pile* and Middle Dutch *pille*, all ultimately from Latin *pilula*, from diminutive of *pila* ball."

As you can imagine, people were thrilled to hear this explanation. By the way, if your clothes do experience pilling, there are any number of clever tools on the market, from clothing razors to sweater stones, for removing them.

The Pocket Check

Before committing any clothes to the washer, check all pockets for coins, tissues, notes, lottery tickets, credit cards and cash. Remember that Canadian dollar bills are plastic and may melt in the dryer, and though I did have a twenty successfully navigate the hot cycle of the washing machine, I wouldn't suggest washing your money either. Also, keep an eye out for jewellery, cell phones, car keys with electronic fobs and small animals. None of these do well in the rinse and spin. If electronic devices do suffer a fall into the laundry tub, you can apparently plop them into a bowl of rice and that will draw the water out (sometimes). I wouldn't count on that, but it's worth keeping in mind.

Preparing the Load for the Washer

If you are worried about an item pilling—not *pulling*—turn it inside out or put it into a mesh bag. Or both. Turn dark jeans inside out too. Yes, the same ones that I told you earlier to put right-side-out when you put them in the laundry basket. Turning darker-on-the-outside clothes inside out will help them resist fading. Okay, so if you want to put dark jeans in the laundry basket inside-out, by all means go ahead.

Let's move on.

Leave shirts unbuttoned. Apparently, all the pushing and pulling that goes on in the washer tub can cause buttons to tear their button-holes. Zip zippers so they don't scrape against other items. Hook hooks so they don't get caught. What happens when a bra hook meets a mesh bag you ask? With all that agitation going on, the snagged items will start twisting, and then a shirt will grab hold and a pair of leggings will join in, and another and another, and then next thing you know you've got one long, tightly twisted conga line of laundry that you have to unwind in order to free it from the machine.

Mind the dryer door for the same reason. If you slam the door on an unsuspecting shirtsleeve— especially one made of stretchy fabric—don't be surprised if you end up with one arm twice as long as other. Oh, and another thing to avoid is accidentally looping a tank top or pair of shorts over the agitator (the giant stirring device in the middle of an older-model washing machine tub). I accidentally did this with a pair of undies, and when I took them out, the left leg hole was twice the size of the waistband. Not a good fit.

How to Load the Washer: Load Size and Composition

You've gathered and sorted, and now you're ready to wash. There's a delicate balance between too many clothes in the washing machine and too few. What we are searching for here is the Goldilocks standard of *just right*.

Don't stuff clothes into the machine. Items need a certain amount of room to move around, to rub against one another (abrasion) and to be sufficiently exposed to the soapy water. Overcrowding can result in clothes not getting fully cleaned, and it can cause excessive rubbing with resultant damage (think of people in a crowded customs line at the airport). "Loosely packed" is what we're aiming for, like a pile of kale in a measuring cup as opposed to tamped-down brown sugar.

Likewise, some experts say small loads do not wash up as well as larger ones because there is too much water and not enough abrasion. This theory holds that any load size smaller than medium is suspect. In my experience, clothes come out clean enough from smaller loads, but they do end up wet-plastered to the side of the washtub in the final spin and therefore come out flat as pancakes. Three white T-shirts and five white socks do not an unwrinkled load make.

What makes up a good load? A medium-to-large pile, with a mix of textures and weights, is a good balance. Towels and bedding are best washed in their own loads.

Balancing the Load

Have you ever heard a peculiar sound coming from the general direction of our laundry room? Slow at first, then quickening and then thundering to a stop: Thuuump. Thump-thump, *thump-thump, thmp-thmp-thmp*. Thuuump. Whomp-whomp-whomp. This would be the washing machine, unbalanced and walking across the floor. Not that it can get very far, trapped as it is between the weighty dryer and the laundry sink. And believe me, that washing machine is heavy, taking more than one solid hip check to get it back into place.

This happens most often with small loads comprising a few heavy items, say a bathmat and a few hand towels. The mat will wend its heavy, soggy way over to one side, throwing the revolving wash tub off its axis, so rather than a smooth spin, it begins to wobble. This will rock the whole machine, and then off it goes. How to remedy this situation? Throw in a few more items to balance the load. Big, not-linting towels are a good bet.

The Order Debate

In researching this book, I repeatedly encountered debate over loading order. Most people suggest adding detergent first, then the laundry and then pulling the dial to start the water flow. Diehard experts advocated a different method: water first, then detergent and other additives (some of which I couldn't even pronounce) and once the tub filled with water, mix well and *then* add the laundry. To which I could only say, "You're kidding, right?"

Detergent, laundry, water is apparently the most common order, but for me this creates a chicken-and-egg problem: How do you really know how big the load is until you get the clothes in the machine? And how do you know how much detergent to add until you know how big the load is? It is this kind of question that leads some launderers to throw up their hands and head to the dry cleaners. *Just do what works for you.* Just don't add bleach at the end lest you end up with spots.

An Ode to Late-Model Washers

Before I go on, let me admit that the order debate has been rendered obsolete by newer machines with a separate compartment for the soap and bleach. Those machines also determine the load size for you, so you have no control over the amount of water added. Energy efficient, they claim. Sadly, in my experience, these machines are wildly inadequate in the one job they were designed to do: clean the clothes. If you have any choice in the matter, *buy an older machine with an agitator.* Or consider going to your local river and scrub your clothes on the big rocks by hand. I swear, your clothes will come out cleaner.

Murphy's Law of Tissue

Eventually, you will wash a tissue. When this happens, your best bet is to carefully remove all items from the machine and into a waiting laundry basket. Wipe the inside of the tub to remove any tissue residue, and then step outside with your basket and prepare to shake the dickens out its contents. Wrist-snapping action is especially effective in detaching tissue fluff and will result in snowstorm-like flurries. These flurries are the reason it is better to be outside the house than inside, where you will end up creating a *Cat in the Hat-*style mess, which will move and expand from one room of the house to the next. Music with a strong bass line played at high volume will also help with your rhythm in the tissue-extraction process, as well as adding a sense of festiveness to the occasion. Once the clothes have been suitably rid of the tissue debris (it may not all come out), shake yourself thoroughly as well to ensure you do not carry any offending white fluff back into the house. Return to the laundry room and throw the clothes in the dryer (while observing good drying practices) and be prepared to scrape remaining tissue from the lint filter and dryer drum.

I hope these bits of advice will help you stay sorted and balanced in the laundry room. Stay tuned for the next exciting instalment in the laundry process: the Cycles of Drying, or Don't Put Your Clothes on the Line When You're Expecting a Tornado. Before we get there, let's pause for a moment of laundry-as-life philosophy.

Don't iron pantyhose.
—Lindy, Aunt Karen's college roommate

Chapter 6

THE TRUTH ABOUT WASHING MACHINES, PERMANENT PRESS AND DELICATES

Minding Your Own Laundry Basket

You can launder more effectively and efficiently if you understand what goes on under the lid of your automatic washing machine when you close it. Most people do not. Many laundry failures and frustrations can be chalked up to the illusion that it is not necessary to know what the different cycles on washing machines do, or why they are recommended for certain fabrics and fibres.

—Cheryl Mendelson, *Home Comforts*

I couldn't agree more. Not that I have ever known anything about the different cycles on our basic two-cycle washing machine. Up until I read about these cycles in Ms. Mendelson's book, I just flipped randomly back and forth between normal/regular and permanent press with, as far as I know, no damage done. Since educating myself as to wash cycles, though, I have been more discriminating in my flipping. I now choose normal/regular for towels, bedding and heavier items, and I pick permanent press for most clothes. Have I seen a difference? Well, no, but I suppose this may be one of those cumulative phenomena the results of which appear only over time and, accordingly, are virtually immeasurable. Reminds me of the kind or not-so-kind ways that we treat other people, or ourselves for that matter. Those effects are cumulative too, one way or the other.

Before I launch off into any laundry-and-love analogies, let's talk about the permanent-press cycle for a moment. I've never actually known what the term permanent press means. It gives the impression that you don't have to iron, that the article of clothing will emerge from the washing machine smooth, crisp and virtually ready-to-wear. Doesn't that sound like a dubious claim? With the sole exception of one pair of pants and a couple of remarkable shirts of Dad's, I've rarely met clothing that resists wrinkling. When I researched the meaning of permanent press, I was indeed met with the alarming proposition that some clothes are chemically treated to resist wrinkles and hold their shape. According to the David Suzuki Foundation, there may be formaldehyde in no-iron shirts too—and *no, they don't put that on the label.*

Formaldehyde? Chemical treatment? How have I not realized this before? But it all makes sense, doesn't it, in this processed world we live in? I am reminded of all the unpronounceable ingredients that are added to food. Apparently, we have *processed clothing* too. And in the interest of fair warning, let me tell you that other words used to indicate permanent-press chemical processing are *no-iron, durable press, wrinkle resistant, wash and wear* and *easy care.* So keep those phrases in mind when you're shopping for clothes. Rather like reading nutritional labels, no?

But I digress. I was telling you about wash cycles. I read in our washing machine's manual that the permanent-press cycle incorporates a special cooling rinse after the wash. It's not clear to me why that would help with wrinkles. Then again, perhaps I should seize on this bit of wisdom and incorporate it into my personal care regimen, spraying my face with cool water after I wash, in an effort to prevent wrinkles.

Now that we have figured out what the permanent-press cycle is, and what clothes it is intended to wash, let's get back to Ms. Mendelson and her illusions.

I smiled when I read the passage about laundry failure arising from folks not understanding their washing machine's cycles. I didn't smile because I was basking in a newfound insight but because it seemed so perpendicular to how our personal relationships work. In my experience anyway. (And yes, I am drawing an analogy between washing machines and relationships. This is what happens when you've spent as much time as I have staring out the window of the laundry room, waiting for the cycle to finish.)

I believe most people have no idea what goes on under the lids of their relationships. What causes a lot of failures and frustrations is the mistaken assumption that they *should* have some idea of what is going on in their relationship, that their relationship should fit tidily into one cycle or the other and that everything should come out, well, *wrinkle-free.* Forget it. Life doesn't work like that. There needs to be room for a lot of compromise and adjustment, *a lot*, rather like the way we sometimes need to mash up our wash loads. We humans have a habit of labelling, categorizing and expecting things and people to operate a certain way. They don't. And you certainly can't hand wash everything, now can you?

By the way: there is no such thing as a permanent-press relationship (or spouse for that matter), notwithstanding what any self-help book tells you.

Speaking of which, when I read further along in *Home Comforts* (Mendelson), I found this little gem: "The type of automatic washing machine that most people in this country have in their homes is a top-loading machine that 'agitates,' or churns or jerks the clothes back and forth, by means of a post in the center of the tub, to wash and rinse them. As it drains the wash and rinses the waters, it spins the clothes at ever-increasing speeds until the great centrifugal force of the spinning presses out so much water that the clothes do not drip—are 'damp dried'—when they are finally removed."

You know where this is going, don't you? Yes, not only do we not know what is going on under the lid of the washing machine, but the wash cycle itself is a handy metaphor for the way relationships operate, churning things up, jerking us about and leaving us feeling as though we have been damp-dried flat. Or so it would seem. If you understand the dynamic, you can avoid getting pilled like a pair of polyester underwear. So how does the wash cycle work exactly? Like this, according to Ms. Mendelson: "Agitation jerks and pulls fabrics. This forces water back and forth through the cloth, dissolving and lifting out dirt. It also abrades—causes a constant rubbing of one item against another—which is part of what gets them clean."

Life works the same way as the wash cycle: We agitate against other people, strangers and loved ones alike. People will often rub us the wrong way. That's okay, because if we pay attention, we will see that the real source of the friction isn't really the other person; it's often a mess in our own fabric that we need to work out. That's good news too, because that is a place where we have some control. Controlling other people? Herding dust bunnies? I wish you luck. So when you are annoyed, take care of yourself, look for your part and remember that blame is as toxic and potent as mishandled bleach.

You can add other materials to the wash load of life too: school obligations, jobs and later on kids, pets and houses. These are all surfactants (substances you add to the wash water that encourages the dirt to loosen and let go). If you're lucky you'll come out of the rinse and spin better for it, liberated from heavy soil and fresh with new insight. It is important to check on the status of stains as you pull items out of the wash. Sometimes stains are set in harder than you realized and you have to treat them again. Or let them sit and soak before trying to loosen them up. (See "Stain Management" and maybe skip the vampire method.) Likewise, pushing down hurt feelings, anger and fear? Not a good idea. These all need fresh air and attention at some point.

And that brings me, finally, to the delicate cycle: "Delicate or gentle laundering is the most variable of the washing machine treatments because the profile of 'delicate' fabrics is so variable. The gentle cycle is needed sometimes because of a garment's fibre content (machine-washable silk and wool, viscose rayon, acrylic and acetate) and sometimes because of its delicate constructions (lace, very sheer fabrics, loosely woven or knitted ones). The slow, short agitation and spin typically used on the delicate cycle offer mechanical protection and reduced abrasion to delicate constructions, weak fibres and fibres that weaken when wet" (Mendelson).

People, like clothing, are made of their own unique fabrics, with varying details, shapes and sizes. In order to avoid being pilled or torn or thrown around like so many socks and soaking wet jeans—which, in an unbalanced washer can cause it to march across the laundry room floor and wreak all kinds of havoc—you have to accept that everyone is constructed differently and treat them, and yourself, accordingly. Dad, for instance, is heavy denim, durable and strong; I, on the other hand, am gossamer, frothy, delicate and easy to tear. Each one of us has our strengths. Together we make a great outfit, but we're not always super compatible in the washing machine. That's okay. It just means we have to pay attention, adjust our expectations and be careful and kind in how we treat each other.

It's the same way with the delicate cycle in the washing machine: "More central to true 'gentle' treatment is gentle agitation. *Agitation does no harm to sturdy cloth, but it can cause pilling on fabrics prone to pilling, as many synthetics are; it can weaken cloth with low abrasion resistance; and it too can result in tearing of extremely delicate fabrics*" (Mendelson; emphasis added).

Low abrasion resistance—of course! The laundry equivalent to being delicate or sensitive. It reminds me of a somewhat emotional discussion your dad and I had many, many years ago. I've forgotten the subject matter, but I remember the last thing he said: "Your sensitivity is overstated."

Right. That's like saying to a piece of chiffon, "Your low abrasion resistance is overstated," meanwhile the chiffon is torn in two. Let this be a lesson in understanding the nature of the fabric and its treatment, in giving the chiffon sufficient space to excuse itself into a mesh bag, or better still, a quick hand wash. *Uh, excuse me while I go for a long drive. Or go to yoga. Or at the very least, hide in the laundry room and do fourteen loads in a row.*

So there you have it. Life, love and laundry. And one last word of advice: mind your own laundry basket.

Postscript: In mid-July, our twenty year old Kenmore washing machine finally gave up, the gearbox having given way under the weight of a load of waterlogged bedding. The agitator seized and would no longer agitate, instead filling the back hall with the smell of burning rubber. So I spent a lot of time with the front-loading machines at the Laundromat up the street (seven of them going at once), and I researched replacements. Nowadays, most models have no agitator at all, lifting and tumbling the laundry by other means. The only problem is these machines have a high-speed spin cycle that can cause clothing to tangle. So agitator or no agitator, things can still get rubbed the wrong way.

Second postscript: In August, our new washing machine arrived, an energy efficient top loader with no agitator. It used very little water, had an impressive digital console and played a charming song to signal the end of the cycle (rather like those annoying Christmas cards that play a high-pitched rendition of "Jingle Bells" as soon as you crack them open). Unfortunately, the new machine didn't get the clothes clean. Disappointed, I ordered a new one, a front loader this time, figuring that gravity would *surely* help in the absence of an agitator. But alas, no. The clothes came out no cleaner. They came out *stinky*. Stinky!

Secretly, I can't wait until this barely-off-the-sales-floor model expires so I can look for an antique one that *actually works*. If I had it to do all over again, I would spend the $750 it would have cost to replace the transmission in our 20-year-old Maytag.

What's the takeaway? Agitation is a good thing, in love and in laundry.

**When in doubt, hand wash
in cold water. Don't take unnecessary risks
with things that are precious to you.**

Chapter 7

DEALING WITH DELICATES

How to Wash Your Cheerleading Uniform

Your cheerleading uniform is important to you. It's custom-made, it's delicate and it's like anything else you value in your life: you treat it with patience, thoughtfulness and loving care. Also, it is expensive and close to irreplaceable, so you sure don't want to fry it in the dryer a week before a competition.

This is the hand-wash method I use, based on a magazine article I cut out a few years ago (then slipped it into a plastic page-protector—the kind with the three holes up the side—which is *perfect* for easy reference. Just install a metal cup hook on the wall and hang all your plastic-encased laundry rules there).

Step 1: Gather your equipment—namely one pail or dish tub (or preferably two), laundry soap (more on that later), rubber gloves (optional), hand moisturizer, hangers and one large bath towel, preferably non-pilling.

Step 2: Lay out the large bath towel on a flat surface beside you (say, for instance, on the top of the washing machine). It is important to have this towel on hand *before* you begin, as you don't want to be scrambling around looking for one at the end of the washing process while holding a dripping garment in your hand, in which case, chances are good you will slop water on the tile floor, slip while you are jumping to grab a towel off the top shelf, land hard on your back and thus end up not being able to wash your uniform at all—or wear it, for that matter—because you'll be in traction instead. So if you don't get a towel ready at the beginning, you may end up with a stinky uniform and a large chiropractic bill.

Step 3: Wash one uniform piece at a time. Or not. But if you do more than one item, make sure you have more than one towel ready too, so you don't end up in traction wearing stinky, unlaundered items as previously explained.

Step 4: Fill a pail or dish tub with cold water. Add a small capful of laundry detergent. It needn't be laundry detergent for delicates. I honestly don't know what the difference is between ordinary laundry detergent and laundry detergent for *delicates*. And while I'm on the subject, is there *really* a difference between the Tide for whites, Tide for cold water and Tide that smells like wildflowers in the springtime? Granted, we know the last one likely causes us to break out in hives, but other than that, why isn't there just one Tide? All this choice could lead a person to question her ability to choose the right detergent and thus to a mental impasse, and a resulting impact on one's happiness and self-esteem. All of which may in turn lead to a questioning of one's ability to, say, serve as a base on an elite cheerleading team, meaning no spandex-and-sequin uniform.

So just use plain Tide.

Step 5: Fill the damn pail with cold water and soap if you haven't already. Give it a stir.

Step 6: If you have a second pail, fill it with fresh water for rinsing. You are going to be at university though, so let's assume you don't have a second pail. Proceed to step 7.

I know, I know: seven steps already, and I haven't even started washing yet?

Listen, laundry is a sacrament. You need to take your time. Close your eyes. Take several deep breaths. Walk a few laps around the laundry room if need be, and then, once suitably calmed, return to your position.

Step 7: If you don't want your hands going numb during the washing and rinsing process, consider pulling on rubber gloves, understanding, of course, that you lose tactile sensation when you do so. Your sense of touch is more important when you are washing *dishes* than clothes, but since this isn't an article about dishes I won't go on about it. So go gloved or not. Your choice. If you don't wear gloves, make sure you have hand cream available for afterward. That's a good idea in any case, as it pays to moisturize one's hands frequently, wouldn't you agree?

Step 8: Plunge the uniform into the soapy water. No, wait. Scratch that. Gently immerse the uniform into the soapy water. Plunging may be too violent an action.

Step 9: Swish the uniform slowly around in the water a few times and then squeeze the suds through the fabric. Pay special attention to the area under the arms where sweat happens. Once the underarm areas have been thoroughly treated, swish the uniform around the pail twice more and then liberate it from the soapy water and ~~plunge~~ ease it into the waiting cold rinse. If you don't have that second pail, this is the point where you ball up the uniform and hold it in one hand while simultaneously dumping the soapy water out of the wash pail, rinsing it thoroughly and refilling it with fresh water. You don't want to be rinsing your uniform in anything less than pure, clear water, so be careful! Otherwise, your uniform may end up with a soapy residue, and who knows what fresh hell that may lead to? Why, your sparkles may detach or something.

Step 10: Thoroughly rinse the uniform in the fresh, cold, uncontaminated rinse water. You might even change the rinse water over the course of the process, depending on how much soap was used in the wash cycle (I did say a small capful, right?). Once satisfied that the uniform has been freed of all soap, lift it slowly and carefully from the rinse water (don't just fling it around) and gently, *gently* squeeze some of the excess water out. Do not wring. Do not squeeze the bejeesus out of it. Do not shake or swing it around your head.

Once the garment has more or less stopped dripping, spread it out flat on the aforementioned large bath towel (you did get one, right?) Then carefully roll the towel up with the garment inside. Once that is done, you can squeeze the towel a bit or heave your own weight over it to encourage more drying. Unroll the towel. Assess dryness of the garment and wetness of the towel. Repeat the process with a fresh towel until the garment is feeling reasonably drip-free dry.

Step 11: Last, either lay the item out on yet another towel and arrange it into its proper shape, or if it is really *quite* dry, hang it up on a hanger to finish. Now, be especially careful with tops if you opt to hanger-dry, because if the garment is too wet or the hanger is the wrong size, it will install shoulders in your uniform that weren't there before. I suppose if you were a slope-shouldered sort, this might be a fine strategy for bulking up your look, but you already have beautifully strong, square shoulders, so do be careful with those hangers.

Step 12: Once fully dry, return the uniform to its place in your closet. Wear with great pride in both your cheerleading capabilities and your hand-washing prowess.

The maintenance of the beauty and quality of your uniform is highly dependent on your patience, commitment and willingness to put in the time to do the job right. Kind of like cheerleading itself, no? (This method also applies to bras or lingerie; items with beading, sequins or other decorative detail that may be yanked off by washer agitation; or other articles of clothing sporting the hand-wash symbol.)

Postscript: other cheer moms have reported that they just toss their daughters' uniforms into the washing machine in the cold cycle and they come out just fine. To each her own.

**To get rid of beet juice stains, put a few drops
of lemon on the spot before you wash it.
—Aunt Arlene, a friend of the family**

**To get rid of beet juice stains, wear an apron.
—Gramper and Juney**

**(or take off your glasses)
—Dad**

Okay, Juney, Gramper and Dad didn't actually say those things,
but we know they're thinking them. I mean, check
out Gramper next time he's having spaghetti!

Chapter 8

TOMATOES, VAMPIRES AND INCONSPICUOUS SPOTS

A Few Thoughts on Stain Management

A few of my earliest childhood memories are marked by food stains.

When I was five, our family attended Sunday services at the United Church on Regent Street, in a little brick building with a big hill in the backyard. One Sunday I wore a pretty white blouse with a plaid kilt and a red sweater. Afterward, we had tomato soup for lunch, which I inevitably spilled all over the front of my blouse. I remember nothing of the incident itself, or the aftermath, but I can still see the orange-red tomato stain on the crisp white cotton, and I can still feel the warm soup cooling quickly against my skin. We didn't go to church too often after that. Maybe it was too much trouble.

Then there was the time I waltzed into our basement rec room with a plateful of spaghetti and executed a perfect pirouette before sitting down to eat. My spaghetti twirled right along with me, flew off the plate and sprayed tomato sauce and pasta all over the white stipple walls and gold carpet. I froze in place, aghast, and then sprinted upstairs to report the incident to Juney and Gramper.

Even as a youngster I understood one of the key tenets of stain treatment: *ya gotta move fast.*

Over the years I've learned a few lessons beyond tomato-stain management (cold water followed by liquid detergent). For one: You don't necessarily need a commercial product like OxiClean or Shout! to tackle a stain. Besides, it's kind of ironic, isn't it? A stain remover called Shout!? Or maybe it just figures that in our society, people think *shouting* is a solution. I am skeptical of miracle products, and increasingly, I don't believe in commercial stain removers, however loud they may be. I do believe in prompt action, careful experimentation and posting what works on a list over the laundry tub.

A few examples? It's a bad idea to use hot water on blood or protein stains because the heat may cook the marks permanently into the fabric. For sweat stains, a combination of vinegar and lemon juice works wonders. Bleach, on the other hand, will darken sweat stains because it reacts with the proteins in perspiration. Besides, bleach is stinky. Laundry detergent and elbow grease work well for mud stains on denim. Rubbing alcohol and paper towels will remove ballpoint pen ink. Lemon juice and sunshine will make whites even whiter, especially sheets. (And hanging sheets outside gets you out into fresh air too, but that's another story.)

When I asked friends for their favourite laundry tips, I learned that everyone has his or her own favourite miracle stain remover, from club soda to hydrogen peroxide to something called Dylon

S.O.S Colour Run (http://www.dylon.com.au/fc-coloursafe.htm). My friend Heidi discovered Dylon S.O.S. in Australia when she accidentally washed a pair of red socks with her regular laundry and everything turned pink. She swears this product saved her clothes, and you know, Heidi is a bank lawyer so she doesn't say things like that lightly. Another friend suggested sucking on fresh blood stains, vampire-like. Apparently, the enzymes in saliva break down the proteins in blood. I don't know. It just seems like bad manners and, well, kind of creepy.

After many years of washing clothes, it seems to me that the fix for stains comes down to a combination of chemistry, timing and patience. With that in mind, here are a few ideas to consider in developing your own stain-management regime:

1. Time: The sooner you deal with a stain, the better. Stains left too long may become permanent.
2. Heat: Heat may set a stain, so avoid using hot water, and do not put the treated item in the dryer until you have made sure the stain has been removed.
3. Friction: Use caution. Rubbing may spread the stain further or may ruin the fabric, especially if it is delicate. Blot a stain instead. Also, work on stains from the reverse side to avoid "pushing" the stain further into the fabric.

It makes sense to consider the type of stain too so you can choose the appropriate solution. This is where chemistry comes into play. Acid neutralizes alkaline, and vice versa. Enzymes break down proteins. Alcohol is a mild solvent, so it works well for dissolving oils. Certain products have oxidizing or bleaching qualities: lemons, vinegar and hydrogen peroxide, for instance. That all makes more sense than shouting at your clothes, doesn't it?

Experimenting with these ideas, you soon learn that some of the best stain removers around aren't found in the laundry aisle. They are found with the baking ingredients (salt, baking soda and vinegar), in the produce section (lemons!) and in the first-aid aisle (alcohol and peroxide). We could add bleach and ammonia to the list, but ever since Dad put those two together, I've avoided keeping them in the same room. By the way, OxiClean? Hydrogen peroxide, give or take a few other ingredients. Either one works well on organic stains like juice, coffee, food, wine and people or pet messes.

Speaking of experiments, no discussion of stains would be complete without mention of the inconspicuous spot test. Except for the bottom of a sock, I am not sure where this alleged *inconspicuous* spot lives. And of course, even the bottom of the sock becomes conspicuous as soon as you relax and put your feet up. Perhaps the better language would be *less conspicuous spot*.

You can always use a stain removal product for convenience sake, but here are a few of my favourite non-commercial stain removing remedies:

In general: A pre-soak will help loosen stains. Hot water is one of the best cleaners around, so wash in the hottest water that is safe for the fabric. Some stains disappear after a single treatment while others may require several trips through the washing machine, so if at first you don't succeed, keep at it.

Sweat stains: combine one cup of vinegar and one cup of lemon juice in a bucket and allow item to soak overnight. How well this works will depend on the fabric.

Oil stains (like olive oil or salad dressing): Blot with rag soaked in alcohol, rinse in cold water and then wash as usual. It might take a few treatments and washings.

Coffee, tea or chocolate: dampen a rag with club soda and blot stain until removed.

Ink: Place paper towel under the stain, and then wet a rag with oxygen bleach, rubbing alcohol or hydrogen peroxide and gently blot spot.

Fruit or wine: douse with lemon juice and allow to dry in the sun (if circumstances permit).

Tomato: rinse with cold water through the back of the fabric and then treat with liquid detergent.

Blood: rinse/soak in cold water and then treat with an enzyme-based product (like OxiClean) or a hydrogen peroxide-based alternative.

As it turns out, off-peak hydro hours (seven p.m. to seven a.m.) are standard for laundry and for writers.

Chapter 9

MY DIRTY LAUNDRY HABITS

The World of Off-Peak Hours and
Outdoor Clotheslines

It all started one grey April morning when I was chatting on the phone with Juney. I was leaning against the kitchen counter, my morning coffee in one hand and the receiver in the other.

"I'll be glad when spring finally gets here," she said. "I'm washing sheets, and it's so much nicer when we can hang them on the line outside."

My ears perked up. With all the laundry research I'd been doing lately, I realized my bed sheet routines were haphazard at best. Juney, on the other hand, was a seasoned veteran. Here was my chance to get the lowdown.

"So, uh, how often do you wash your sheets?" I asked, trying to sound matter-of-fact.

"Usually I do the bedding once per week," she said, "but in the summer, I might wash the sheets twice because they smell so good when they've been hung on the line."

Twice? In one week?

I stared out the kitchen window. I am quite sure I could count on two hands, maybe less, the number of times I wash bedding *in a year*. I can trace my erratic linen laundering practices back to a paragraph in a mothering manual I read long ago: "The busy mother of a young family may safely rely on the time-honoured tradition of pulling back the quilt and airing the sheets between launderings." Never mind that I may have *read in* the concept that airing sheets was a *substitute* for washing them. It was that magical phrase—"time-honoured tradition"—that gave me license to relax, a licence I seized upon with such ferocity that it became embedded in, well, our household bedding.

There is a catch to the sheet-airing method of bed-linen maintenance though, something I haven't mentioned to my mother. Well, not a catch, exactly, but rather a *cat*. Mazey, our beloved tortoise-shell tabby, can sense exposed bedding from any location in the household and will immediately sprint up the stairs and insinuate herself into the airing process, thus leaving a residue of cat fur all over the exposed sheets. I expect cat fur on the exterior bedding, the quilt or duvet—that's part of the deal with cats—but to have fur on top of *and* in the bed is a stretch even for a cat lover like me. To avoid this, I've resorted to yanking back the duvet and vigorously flicking the sheets a few times. A speed-airing of sorts. I have to execute this motion quickly or lock Mazey out of the room, because she thinks all of this sheet flicking is a game I devised especially for her.

Needless to say, Juney doesn't own any cats.

And now, here she was telling me she *washed* her linens as often as twice a week. I stood there with the receiver to my ear, sheets flapping on a clothesline in my mind, when she came out with a one-two punch. "Using the clothesline really saves on electricity," she said.

"Huh. I can see that it would."

"And I like to save using the dryer for off-peak hours."

Off-peak?

"You know," she said, perhaps realizing I didn't know at all. "After seven p.m."

I was vaguely aware that the cost of electricity varied with the time of day, but I'd never given it any thought. I'd always used both the dryer and the hot water wash cycle whenever it suited me, with no regard whatsoever to hydro rates. I paused to consider the cost of indiscriminate drying, and later, when I looked up the variable hydro rates online, I was staggered to read that 5 to 10 percent of domestic electricity use is directly attributable to household dryers. People cut their electric bills in half just by managing their time of use. Our electric bills can run to a few hundred dollars each month. *I could cut that cost by as much as half?*

All this talk of hydro rates, off peak hours and fresh sheets got me thinking. Juney always had an outdoor clothesline. So did her mother. Why didn't I have one? I mean, *clotheslines are really fun.*

When I was a kid, we had a pulley-style clothesline that stretched from the back porch to a hydro pole on the other side of the yard. I used to grab onto it with both hands and then launch myself off the wooden railing, zip-line style, swinging wildly over the lawn until my progress stalled about halfway out, the clothesline sagging in the middle, and then I'd drop down to the grass below. Nowadays, Juney has one of those square metal contraptions that sits on a steel post, umbrella-like, with lines of white nylon running in neat rows from one side of the frame to the other. It's the same kind of clothesline my grandmother had when she lived in the centre of town. My grandmother's line stood in her side yard, a maze of sheets and pillowcases that I would bat my way through, grass and dandelions tickling my bare feet. It was like a magic door between the grassy hill of her front yard and the rocky garden, full of snapdragons and sweet peas in the back.

"You have always had clotheslines, haven't you?" I asked Juney, even though I knew the answer.

"Yes," she said. "I'll bet your dad would help you install a line if you wanted one."

Well, of course I wanted one. There was really no choice, you see. Between the lure of fresh-smelling sheets, the potential hydro savings, the nostalgic pull of family tradition and now the offer of free help, a clothesline was a no-brainer.

"Thanks, Mom," I said. "I'll take a look around the yard and figure out where I can set one up."

I could hear Gramper's voice saying something in the background.

"Dad says to be careful about what kind you buy," she said. *More mumbling.* "And he'll show you how to store it properly."

"Sounds good," I said. I hung up and considered my next move.

Since it was April, and a wet one at that, installing an outdoor clothesline would have to wait. But I could make a change right away by observing off-peak hydro hours. This wasn't as easy as it sounds. Laundry is an itch I would scratch the moment I woke up and keep scratching all morning long, which, in the wintertime it turns out, is *peak hours*, meaning the hydro rate was almost double what it would be if I could restrain myself until after seven p.m. It was a hard habit to break, the pull of laundry in the morning being akin to the pull of coffee. Believe it or not, it took a considerable fit of self-discipline *not* to run three loads before nine a.m. (Peak hydro hours run seven-to-noon in April, *sigh*.)

I know what you're thinking: Mom, are you admitting you have a laundering addiction?

Well, not exactly.

I do have a deeply engrained habit of getting laundry done in the morning, weaving it around my office work. You know how good it feels to stroke items off your to-do list? That little positive charge of *got that done!* It's like that, and to stroke three loads off the list first thing in the morning is a happy way to start the day. Before I go too far down this road of My Morning Laundry Addiction, let me say this: the lure of saving money, of setting a good example for my daughters, *that* was enough of a reward to cure me. And here's something else I discovered: doing laundry and writing in the evening makes for a great combination, the pull of the dryer keeping me from calcifying in my chair.

But mastering off-peak was only half the battle. The next step was the outdoor clothesline.

So what did I do? The only sensible thing anyone ever does in such circumstances: I called my mother back. I can do all the online research I like, but that only ends up with my thinking that I need to buy a top-of-the-line kit from Australia. Meanwhile, my parents have 50 years of experience. Why reinvent the clothesline when I can borrow theirs?

I called Gramper from the laundry section of the local hardware store. I was doing some preliminary scouting and wanted his opinion.

"Don't buy the one that looks like an upside-down umbrella," he said right off. "The lines get shorter and shorter as you make your way toward the middle. It just gets useless for hanging anything."

I hesitated. The umbrella version had 14 feet more line than the giant-T version he was recommending.

"Don't do it," he said. "Come over to our house and look at ours."

"Mm-hmm," I replied, looking at the fancy box. One hundred ninety-six feet is a lot of extra line.

"Come over here now and look the one we have. Do you have time?"

Of course I had time, and I knew he had a point. Lots of times buying the more expensive version in the fancy box with the pictures isn't a guarantee of better quality or functionality. Lots of times, how something looks on display isn't how it will look six months later, either.

But 196 extra feet.

I shook it off. "Yes, I have time. I'll be there soon."

I took pictures of the boxes and then hustled myself out of the store, into my van and straight to my parents' house. When I arrived, they were both outside dressed in their gardening clothes.

"I've been moving shrubs," Gramper said, wiping his hands of top soil. "Come on out back. I'll show you."

Sure enough. He was absolutely right, and I did have to see it to fully appreciate the explanation. The way the umbrella version was strung, the rows of clothesline gets progressively shorter as you moved toward the middle until, once you reached the centre, the hanging space might be all of a foot and a half in length. Useless for anything but one pair of panties and a sock. My parents' line, on the other hand, was strung in perfect parallel lines, one ten-foot row of glorious drying space after another. Why, this would easily be three times as much space as I currently work with indoors.

We discussed the installation process—a tube and cement to anchor the pole in the ground, the three-part support pole and the need for an augur, hand-powered, not electric. He gave me careful instructions about winter storage, about tying the lines together just so.

"Otherwise," he said, pointing at the lines, "they cross over each other and get all tangled up, and it's a helluva mess."

You disregard advice like this at your peril.

Once installed, I will have my first load of off-peak bed sheets flapping in the breeze, cat-fur free, getting bleached by the summer sun.

It's a revolution, I tell you.

It's you turning into your parents, you might say.

Perhaps so. It's a cycle either way, is it not?

Don't put your clothes on the line when you're expecting a tornado.

Chapter 10

HOW TO INSTALL A CLOTHESLINE

Even Though I Haven't Installed One Myself. Yet.

Before you invest in a clothesline, you will need to figure out where you are going to put it, how much space you have available and what style will work.

Step 1: Placement

Whites love the sun. Darks and bright colours do not love the sun and may fade. A slightly breezy area is ideal, though too much wind, as can happen in our yard, may lead to your panties ending up in the pine trees. There are also issues of privacy and consideration of your neighbours' view.

Step 2: Styles

As you assess the situation, keep in mind that there are lots of different kinds including the T-pole, the umbrella, the line-and-pulley and the retractable.

Step 3: Quality, Cosmetics and Price

I read about flimsy support poles (buy steel, not aluminum, and what about bamboo?) as well as lines kinking, sagging, stretching and fraying. "Does not hold up beach towels," one online review noted. Will it hold up in strong winds? Can you tuck it away or fold it down? Consider how it will look cosmetically too. Will it fit in with the garden gnomes? What will the neighbours think (and who cares unless you have Homeowner Association regulations tying up your laundry line)?

Step 4: Installation

The steps involved will vary with the type, but don't hesitate to *call your grandfather*. Or your mother. Possibly both. Not because you are not fully competent to do this job yourself, but because it pays to leverage the experience (and mistakes) of others. Failing that, read the instructions carefully, measure twice and install once. If you want to get fancy, you can add little key rings to your line to permit hanging the orderly and secure placement of hangers for drying shirts (and yes, that is your grandfather's idea).

Step 5: Supplies, Maintenance, Storage and Usage Notes

- Consider where and how to store clothes pegs. You'll want them close at hand.

- The lines get dirty over time and will need to be wiped with a damp cloth from time to time, and no, rain doesn't help.
- Plan to tuck your clothesline away in the wintertime. Granted, the squirrels may miss it. How to store it will depend on the type, but mind that the lines do not get tangled.

It really does make a difference if you shake out the clothes before you put them in the dryer.
—Helen Murray, neighbour

Chapter 11

CYCLES OF DRYING

Around and Around We Go

The drying cycle is the big finale of The Laundry Show. At least it is in our house, since I do not believe in ironing. To kick off the dryer cycle, let's start with three basic principles.

First, as a general rule (towels excepted), don't fry things to a crisp in the dryer. It is hard on your clothes and wastes electricity.

Second, pay attention. The dryer can be your friend and ally in terms of reviving just-washed clothes to a delightfully unwrinkled state. It can also wreak havoc, whether by installing wrinkles where none belong or by shrinking your favourite cotton Capri pants two sizes too small.

Third, and as a corollary to the first two rules, whenever possible, hang stuff up.

I realize that hanging stuff up will pose a challenge for you while living in a university residence. Optimal drying requires space for a clothesline or at least a drying rack. Having traveled with me in Europe, you'll also know that you can get mighty creative about where and how you can hang up at least a few freshly washed clothes.

There are all manner of other exciting topics to cover, from drying flat to letting it all hang out in the wind, so let's dig in.

To Dryer or Not to Dryer: Item by Item Dryer Guidelines

What Not to Put in the Dryer: Items made from manmade fibres like Lycra, nylon and spandex, and include gym shorts and sports tops, bras and underwear, some socks and most yoga clothes. Any item that you've hand washed should also be spared the heat. If an item doesn't like the washer, it probably doesn't like the dryer either.

What to Fluff: Fluffing refers to a short spin in the dryer intended to initiate the drying process, ease out wrinkles and soften up clothing before hanging them up to finish. I fluff blouses, T-shirts and tanks, as well as pants and shorts made of lighter materials, letting them spin until they are three-quarters dry. Cotton underwear does well with a light fluffing too, but not too long since the dryer is not kind to elastic waistbands.

What to Dry: Clothing made of heavier materials, such as jeans, cords and heavy sweatshirts can stand a longer dry time.

What to Bake: Towels and sheets can be thoroughly baked in the dryer. Towels, in particular, need to be 100 percent dry before you fold them and put them away, failing which they may become mildewed and stinky. If you are a laundry idealist, you can also skip the dryer and hang these outdoors on a clothesline—you know, for the few days of summer we actually have in Canada.

Wildly Inappropriate but Soul-Nourishing Dryer Use

I love the feel of towels pulled fresh from the dryer, especially in the wicked cold of mid-January when any source of heat is welcome. Some folks actually have towel-heating racks in their bathrooms so there are always warm-baked towels close at hand. Not me. I just throw the towels in the dryer for ten minutes, roll them up tightly to conserve the heat and then stack them on the bathroom vanity beside the shower. That way, when I turn off the water, I can grab a fistful of warmth from behind the shower curtain and thereby brace myself against the frigid air of the bathroom in winter. Yes, it is wildly wasteful of electricity, but these are the sorts of allowances one makes in order to survive a harsh Canadian winter.

Now, let's get back to the how-to task at hand and load the dryer with *wet* clothes in place of dry towels.

Dryer Loading Method

Check any items you treated for stains. If the stains haven't fully lifted, then re-treat the stain and return the item to the wash pile or, at the very least, don't put it in the dryer.

If you're not in a hurry, shake each item lightly before putting it into the dryer. No, this wasn't my idea. A neighbour suggested it.

"It really does make a difference," she wrote to me in an email, "if you shake clothes out before putting them in the dryer."

"You shake *every item* out between the washer and the dryer?" I asked when I ran into her at the mailbox. I thought I spent a lot of time in the laundry room, but this shaking-out business must add several minutes to every load.

"Yes, pretty much," she said, "though I don't really bother with socks and underwear."

Well, that's a relief.

I've always shaken out clothing and towels when I've taken them out of the dryer, but I never thought to do it *before* putting them in to dry. I've tested this method since, and I can't really tell if it has improved the situation, but perhaps my experiment has not been of sufficient duration. Admittedly, I've wondered whether there is any placebo effect going on in my neighbour's laundry room (and I have no argument with that).

As with the washer, dryer loads need to be of a certain size in order for the dryer to work effectively. If the dryer is not at least one-third full, the items will end up plastered against the sides of the drum like long flat pancakes, misshapen and seriously wrinkled. If you do not have enough items, you can toss in a couple of large towels. (There's those dry towels going back in the dryer again!)

Finally, I do believe in an authoritative shaking out of items as they exit the dryer, meaning a little wrist snap action as opposed to wet-dog action, in order to disburse any recalcitrant wrinkles. This really does make a difference.

Dryer Maintenance: Lint and Heat Do Not Mix

Lint + high heat = fire hazard. Therefore, you must clean the dryer's lint filter regularly. An old toothbrush comes in handy for this job. (Come to think of it, old toothbrushes are so handy that they deserve a whole book of their own.)

Incidentally, did you know that there is a whole Wikipedia article on lint? I kid you not. It covers, among other things, dryer lint, pocket lint and navel lint. *No, really!* Apparently, navel lint is also known as "navel fluff, belly-button lint, belly-button fluff and dip lint" and is technically defined as "an accumulation of fluffy fibres in the navel cavity." What does belly-button lint have to do with laundry? Nothing, but it seemed too important not to include here. I recommend against using the toothbrush for removal of belly-button lint though. *Ouch!*

Drying Racks

A drying rack can be an official bought-for-the-purpose device (the styles and designs of which are too numerous to fully cover here), or can be as simple and off-the-cuff as the back of a chair if you are tight on space. I favour a wooden accordion-style rack because it is space-efficient. These only work for hanging items up though; they don't work for flat-drying sweaters. For that, you can fake it with a giant towel, like I do, or you can invest in flat racks made of tight-knit mesh stretched over a square wire frame (some are even stackable). These optimize air circulation, meaning quicker drying times and less chance of damp-stink invading your clothes. Heaven forbid we have damp-stink. The key to drying sweaters and other knits is to carefully arrange the article back into its proper shape, smoothing out any ripples and making sure the fabric isn't bunched or stretched. Failure to do so can result in your clothing taking on unexpected angles or lengths.

Clotheslines and You

I realize the following advice may not apply until you have occasion to buy or rent a house. I have included it anyway, to ensure you are receiving the broadest possible education in laundry (besides, I might forget later). Using a clothesline saves on hydro, minimizes wear and tear on your clothes, avoids shrinkage and is a great stretching opportunity for those of us who spend too much time hunched over our computers. Here are a few thoughts on how to best line-dry clothes whether indoors or outdoors.

What Not to Line Dry

- Any item with a care tag that reads "dry flat" or has a square symbol with a hyphen in the middle. And may I just say, "Who designs these care label symbols, anyway?" Because that one looks like a filing-cabinet drawer.
- Stretchy clothing items, such as or knit sweaters or long-sleeved T-shirts made with Lycra or nylon. The extra weight caused by the moisture in the fabric may cause these items, if hung, to get longer *and longer*, eventually turning into clothes reminiscent of Dr. Seuss's "thneeds" (those weird onesies the Lorax fought so hard against).

Hanging Tips

- Hang clothes so their shape is maintained. No bunching up! This will speed drying and minimize the risk of mildew.
- Don't crowd clothes either. Allow a little space between them.
- Support it, support it, support it! Use as many clothes pins as necessary to maintain the items' proper shape. Don't allow clothes or towels to sag like thin, soggy Parisian pizza crust.
- Pants will dry well pinned at the waist, or by matching the inner seams and hanging them upside down by their hems, legs together.
- Shirts and blouses are best hung by their hems or by using a hanger that properly fits the shirt (an improper fitting hanger will install shoulders where there weren't any before). Incidentally, this is why it is a good idea to have a few different shapes and sizes of hanger on hand.
- Socks should be hung to dry in pairs. Trust me: it just makes it easier to match them up later.
- Sheets are best hung by folding them in half and hanging them by the matched hems, using as many pins as necessary to avoid sheet sag. If you hang a sheet by its middle, you may end up with an *unsightly* crease (not that anyone will ever see it once it is on the bed and buried beneath the blankets and duvet. But *you* will know).

Flouting Convention by Using an Outdoor Clothesline

When I was a kid, you could stand on the back porch in the summertime and see a parade of clean laundry in one backyard after another all the way down the street. *Everybody* had an outdoor clothesline. In the last few decades, that tradition seems to have vanished, especially in newer neighbourhoods like ours. Built in the early 1990s, our subdivision didn't permit clotheslines because of rules that ran with the property, rules that purported to maintain a certain standard of *how things look* as opposed to *how to best get the job done.* I suppose that even now some people may be offended at the sight of their neighbours' boxer shorts, panties and bras fluttering in the wind.

Here are a few thoughts on effective clothesline use:

- If you are hanging clothes outside, mind the weather. Don't put your clothes on the line when you're expecting a tornado, thunderstorm, rain shower, hail, sleet or pestilence. In other words, there are only about five days in July when you can expect to be able to use your outdoor line.
- Small children with cherry popsicles also pose perils to fresh laundry, as do crop dusters and weed sprayers (organic or not), birds and flying squirrels. You should also be prepared for the neighbour two doors down to start a bonfire without any notice to you. Don't say I didn't warn you.

- Check for stowaways when you bring the clothes back inside. Aunt Karen reports that as a child, she often had to bring the laundry in from the outdoor clothesline. "You'd have to give them a good shake," she said, "in case any bugs landed and wheedled their way into a sleeve or pant leg." It's also a good idea to check for bird poop.

No clothing was harmed in the writing of this book.

**The washing machine, however, did not survive a load of quilts and bedding.
RIP Maytag Model LAT9206.**

Chapter 12

A RAT'S NEST IN THE DRYER VENT

A Cautionary Tale on the Importance
of Regular Maintenance

It all starts with the tennis balls.

"Well, they're not exactly tennis balls," I say to Juney as we stand beside the washer and dryer in our Florida condo.

I flip open the lid of the cardboard box I'm holding: *100% Wool Dryer Balls*. I grab one and toss it up in the air.

"They sure look like tennis balls," Juney says, looking doubtful. She pulls the lint filter from its slot in the top of the dryer and sets about cleaning it with a toothbrush.

I plop the ball back into the box and tuck the lid closed. "The last time I was here I noticed that it took forever for stuff to dry in the dryer, so I thought maybe these would help. Can't hurt to try them out."

"Yes, I've noticed that too," Juney says. She taps the last of the dust off the filter and slides it back into place. "Maybe the dryer vent needs cleaning—the one in the back of the machine that sends the hot air outside."

It had never occurred to me that there might be a connection between the dryer's *not drying* and a clogged exhaust vent.

"Shall we do it right now?" Juney asks.

Dressed in her green squirrel pyjamas and a pink-and-white robe, Juney's been washing and drying loads of bed linens since early in the morning. She was about to transfer a load of beach towels from the washer to the dryer when I showed up with the dryer balls.

"Sure," I say. "Why not?"

The dryer is wedged between the washer and a cement wall, so there isn't much room to move. I grasp one front corner of the machine with both hands and heave on it with all my body weight, inching it forward one diagonal step. I grab the opposite corner and yank it forward too, one side and then the other, wrestling that beast of a machine—which outweighs me at least threefold—away from the wall. Then I jump up onto the top of the machine and prepare to hop down behind it but am stopped, stock-still, on my perch. Below me, the exhaust tube has pulled off the back of the dryer and dropped away. I blink and lean sideways to get a better look. It's all I can do to keep my balance.

Is that *straw* sticking out of the back of the dryer? And not just a few odd bits but a bundle, a thick fistful, *stuffed* into the exhaust space.

I feel momentarily faint. In my mind, I see flames shooting out the back of the dryer, crawling up the wall, into to the rag-filled cupboards and licking up toward the ceiling to threaten the bedroom above. A shiver runs up my spine. I close my eyes and shake away the image.

"Holy cow," I say. "Holy freakin' cow."

Or should I say rat? A holy mouse perhaps?

Yes, an entire rodent's nest is in the back of the dryer. We've had a family of roof rats in the attic recently, but apparently our rat relocation service didn't check the dryer vent. How long has the nest been there? How is it we haven't had a fire? How did I, master of all things home maintenance, allow that to happen? Is there a warning about this in the dryer manual? Wait, have I ever even read the manual? I have a three-story fire-escape ladder and two fire extinguishers, but I didn't think to read the dryer manual?

I jump backward off the top of the dryer. "Mom! You've got to see this!"

Juney peeks over the top of the dryer, her mouth falling open, aghast. "Good heavens," she says and then backs away. "I'll get your dad."

Gramper joins us moments later, his hair sticking up, shaving cream remnants on his cheeks. The three of us swing into action, gathering gloves, a plastic bag, the shop vac, a broom and dustpan. Gramper trouble-shoots the process as I crawl over the back of the dryer and consider my first move.

"Are you okay back there?" he asks. "You don't have a lot of room. Do you need an extension cord? What about a wire brush?"

"I'm good, Dad," I say, setting my shoulders and exhaling.

He peeks over the back of the dryer and hands me a vacuum tool with a brush attachment. "You'll need this," he says.

"Thanks," I say, accepting it from him. Usually he's the one in charge and I'm handing him the tools.

I pull a fistful of material—a cozy nest of straw and dryer lint—out of the vent and drop it into the waiting plastic bag, grateful not to be pulling out any live animals with it. I run the shop vac hose into the back of the dryer as far as it will reach and then check inside with my gloved hand. I vacuum every speck of dust from the back of the machine, the inside of the silver hosing and the vent in the wall, check every crevice carefully by hand, and then vacuum it again, and once more for good measure. (And throughout this exercise, may I stress that the dryer was, indeed, unplugged.)

"They must have gotten in there when you're away in the off-season," Gramper says.

"Yeah, you're probably right," I say, mentally adding yet another item to our seasonal check-in list.

"We'll need to fix the exterior exhaust so it's harder for them to get in," he adds. "That'll be a bugger of a job."

"Yup," I say, pulling off my gloves. "Would you hand me the duct tape so I can fix this hose? It's got a tear in it."

Gramper wonders aloud if we need a trip to Home Depot to replace the now-torn exhaust pipe. He hands me the tape roll.

"Maybe," I say. "This'll do for now." I tear off a strip of tape and carefully cover the open section, admiring my handiwork as I tighten the metal strapping to fix it back in place. Then I clamber back over the top and body-check the dryer back into place. Juney loads the bed linens into the dryer, checks the dial settings and closes the door.

Forty-five minutes after she presses the start button, we have fresh, dry sheets. With no mice or rats.

So what did I learn? To thank the laundry angels for not allowing our house to burn down as a result of my neglect, and to forgive myself for not being born a walking encyclopaedia of laundry appliance care. Oh, and the wool dryer balls? Worked like a charm, though maybe their impact was exaggerated by the liberation of the exhaust pipe.

Short Instructions on Dryer Maintenance

When you own your own dryer one day, you will want to be aware of the following instructions. They may also come in handy if you feel inspired to cross-examine the university maintenance folks who are charged with servicing the laundry equipment.

1. Read the manual!
2. Clean the lint filter *every time you use the dryer.* Use a toothbrush as necessary to remove any stubborn bits. Replace the filter if it has any tears in it. The lint filter is located either on the top of the dryer or in the door.
3. Vacuum out the lint filter housing every few months. That's the place where the lint filter sits. Unplug the dryer when you are doing this. A healthy respect for electricity is a good thing.
4. At least once per year, remove the vent from the back of the dryer and clean the hose all the way out to the duct vent hood. Yes, I will get you your own special brush for this

purpose. Check the hose more often if you suspect rodents or if your dryer isn't getting the job done.

5. If you are unclear on any aspect of this process, get a veteran's advice. If you ever have the household-appliance guy around the house on a repair, ask for his input. You can also look for instructional videos on the internet, provided you give due attention to the credibility and reliability of the source.

6. Above all, *be thee wary of the rat's nest in the dryer vent.*

Irony.
The opposite of wrinkly.

Chapter 13

TAKING YOUR LAUNDRY SHOW ON THE ROAD

Washing Clothes While Traveling Abroad

We've traveled a lot over the years and, as you will know, having a few laundry tricks tucked in your baggage can help keep the trip stay fresher-smelling.

You've learned this first-hand. You've had a showdown with the laundry-on-the-road demons and you have survived. You spent two weeks in Ecuador on a school-building mission trip and a week in Orlando with your cheerleading team. *All without your mother.* As I recall, your mission work socks took on their own special brand of stinky that grew ranker with every passing day (but since all your friends' socks were equally stinky, you didn't really care). You recollected how you would air-dry those socks by sticking your feet over the side of the boat as you traveled up-river to your work site.

Traveling in the Amazon taught you the power of *quick-drying clothes*—fabrics with nylon, Lycra or spandex. You know the ones.

They emerge from the washing machine virtually dry with nary a wrinkle. These allow for the least amount of laundry effort and the most efficient drying. Travel will also have taught you another key tip: layering! Not just for efficient temperature management but also for laundering. If you wear a T-shirt under your sweater, you can often get away with washing that light under-layer and spare yourself the heavier outer one.

You've observed me in laundry action during our family travels to Europe too. We visited London, Paris, Madrid and Rome with romps through the countryside in each place, squashing ourselves and our carry-on luggage in rented compact European automobiles. I didn't pack laundry detergent. Like a lot of things in life, I made it up as we went along.

The only city where we had proper laundry facilities was London (if you consider confusing, high-energy-efficient but deadly slow German washers and dryers to be proper). In every other country I was left to devise a method of laundering on the fly, and since most of these treks included a road trip with new hotels on a daily basis, there was a constant change in laundry facilities (laundry facilities meaning sink, shower, towels. Perhaps the back of a chair to serve as a drying rack). Whenever we cracked opened the door to a new hotel room, I would immediately stick my head in the bathroom and assess the laundry situation. The second thing I would do was to locate soap and start the day's wash in order to maximize available drying time.

You may think back on those trips and remember *baguette, Big Ben* and *pasta Bolognese;* I remember how to pronounce "laundry soap" in three languages:

- **Parisian French**—*lessive,* sometimes with *fraîcheur alpine.* This is to be contrasted with Québécois French, wherein it is expressed, predictably, as *un détergent.*
- **Spanish** *jabón de lavar*—where the *j* is pronounced with that breathy *h* sound, adding a sense mystery and foreign intrigue.
- **Italian** *sapone da bucato*—which sounds like an appetizer, but then so do most words in Italian.

If we didn't have laundry soap, I would resort to shower gel or shampoo, filling the basin with water, squeezing a dollop into the running water and then stirring it around with my hand. One by one I would dunk each item, squeeze the suds through and finish with a cold rinse in the shower.

The drying cycle consisted of gently wringing out excess water, rolling each item in a towel and finding a place to hang it up. European hotels are rather stingy with towels, not to mention hotel-room space, so I would do a small load every day, knowing space for drying would be extremely limited. I would use every conceivable hanging device I could find: coat hangers, chair backs, the shower bar if there was one and in one glorious case, a bunk-bed frame. Navigating the room could become a bit of an obstacle course once the laundry was hung, especially at night, when an innocuous trip to the bathroom might result in a wrestling match with a damp blouse hung from a doorframe. Where possible, I would engage sunlight by hanging items as near to a window as possible (this doesn't work well in England). On the other hand, I used air conditioners or heaters sparingly and with great caution, not wanting to start an unintentional bonfire in the hotel room.

Once suitably dried, I would shake the board stiffness out of the clothes and hand-fluff the items back to life. And then the cycle would start all over again. Pretty much immediately.

In fairness, I should share your father's on-the-road laundering method. He just steps into the shower with his clothes on, lathers up, rinses and hangs to dry (the clothes, not himself). I can't comment on the success of this method, having never tried it, and we all know Dad's standards as to cleanliness and neatness are a little different from mine. I suppose we could have used the save-our-laundry-and-find-a-Laundromat approach, but somehow that never figured its way into our GPS.

So there you have it: our combined foreign laundry experiences collected in one place. May you always have clean underwear. May you always have reasonably fresh clothes when you're on the road and may you remember how to keep them that way without a lot of effort. And may you have many happy travels no matter how stinky your socks get.

CLOTHING REPAIRS: A FLOW CHART

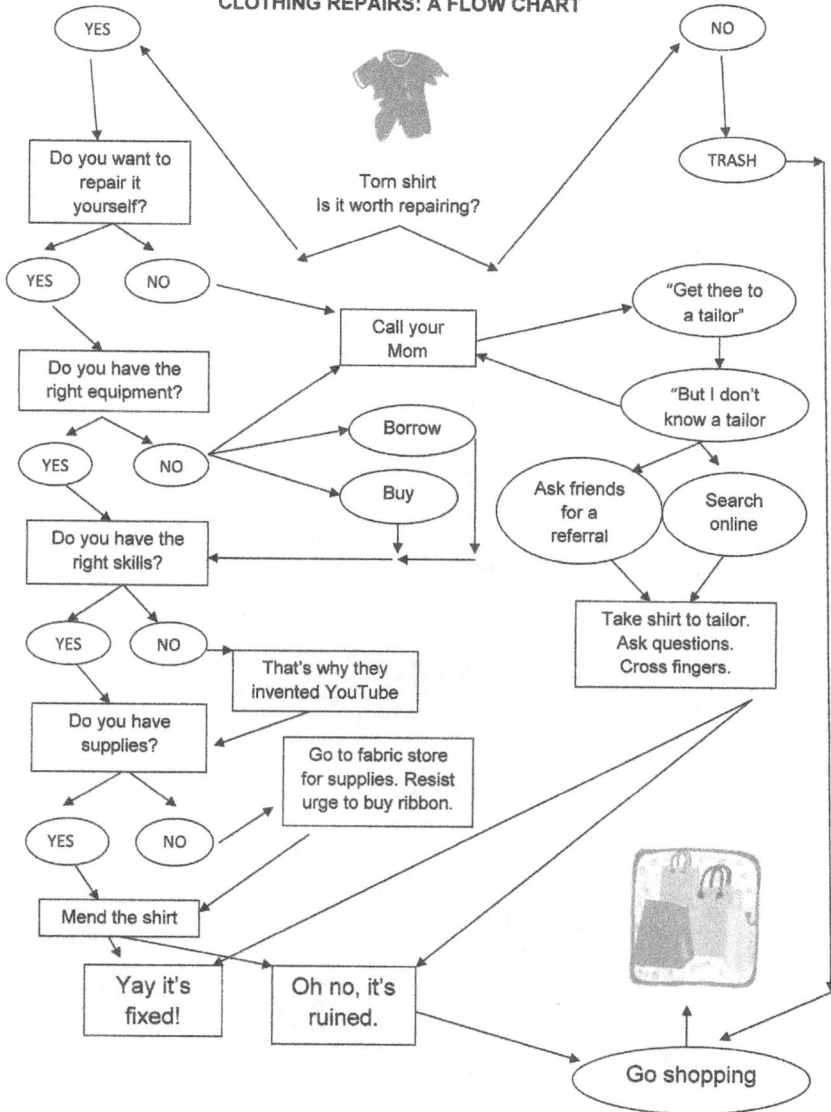

Torn shirt
Is it worth repairing?

YES → **Do you want to repair it yourself?**

NO → TRASH

Do you want to repair it yourself?
- YES → **Do you have the right equipment?**
- NO → **Call your Mom**

Do you have the right equipment?
- YES → **Do you have the right skills?**
- NO → Borrow / Buy

Call your Mom → "Get thee to a tailor"

"Get thee to a tailor" → "But I don't know a tailor"

"But I don't know a tailor"
- Ask friends for a referral
- Search online

Ask friends for a referral / Search online → **Take shirt to tailor. Ask questions. Cross fingers.**

Borrow / Buy → **Do you have the right skills?**

Do you have the right skills?
- YES → **Do you have supplies?**
- NO → **That's why they invented YouTube**

That's why they invented YouTube → **Do you have supplies?**

Do you have supplies?
- YES → **Mend the shirt**
- NO → **Go to fabric store for supplies. Resist urge to buy ribbon.**

Go to fabric store for supplies. Resist urge to buy ribbon. → **Mend the shirt**

Mend the shirt
- **Yay it's fixed!**
- **Oh no, it's ruined.**

Take shirt to tailor. Ask questions. Cross fingers.
- **Yay it's fixed!**
- **Oh no, it's ruined.**

Oh no, it's ruined. → **Go shopping**

TRASH → **Go shopping**

Stains aren't dirt. They are inadvertent dyings.
—Cheryl Mendelson, *Home Comforts*

Chapter 14

ADDITIVES AND BOOSTERS

Recommended Reading

I had never heard of additives and boosters before I began writing this book for you. I knew about stain treatments and bleach, of course, but bluing, borax and trisodium phosphate were new to me. These products, I read, help deodorize, loosen stains, soften the wash water, act as a buffer and prevent the redeposit of soil.

Surely we want to prevent the redeposit of soil, wouldn't you agree?

As I read about these products, it got me thinking about my own additives and boosters, and how those might be the most important words of advice I could share with you. What helped me through my own rinse and spin cycles? What helped prevent the redeposit of nasty moods once I'd managed to loosen them? What have my buffers been? Here are a few:

- **Exercise**—the single best antidepressant and mood elevator ever invented. Wait a minute. Exercise—moving our bodies—is not *invented* at all, is it? It's natural. Maybe that's why it works so well?

- **Time to Myself** —Whether I'm taking a walk, going for a drive or "hiding out" in the laundry room, time to oneself is a great restorative. Our souls aren't meant to be with other people 24/7, no matter how much we love them.

- **Music**—The right beat can get us going in the morning, lift our spirits when we're feeling low or inspire us to pick up the pace in the gym. And a well-written lyric can help reconnect us to the world by showing us we're not alone, that someone else has been in our shoes, that we are part of something larger. After all, *we are the champions … of the world!* Or perhaps just the laundry room.

- **Meditation and Mindfulness**—These practices—learning to watch our thoughts and to work with them—empower us to break free of negative thinking and ugly emotional cycles. They allow us to see the world, ourselves and others more clearly, and in a compassionate light. This, in turn, allows us to act both more sensibly and more kindly toward others and ourselves.

- **Sharing Conversation**—with people who listen well and shares of themselves in return: enough said!

And then there are books. Books may be the most powerful buffer of all for me—life-brightening, colour-boosting, energy-reviving phosphates for the soul. So what follows are some titles from my sacred stack. They're like friends I return to again and again, books that have changed how I see people, myself, the world and my place in it. They helped me realize my responsibility for my lot in life and my responsibility to you.

Here are a few of my favourites:

Love Is Letting Go of Fear by Gerald Jampolsky: I picked up *Love is Letting Go of Fear* when I was in law school, at a book fair in the student centre at York University. I was 21 years old, one of the youngest in my law-school class, and I had just broken up with my high-school boyfriend of three years, John (tall, athletic John with the curly jet-black hair). It was early April, the weather grey and lousy and I was mired in a depression so deep that every day felt like slogging through cement in hip waders. If I'd gone to a clinic at the time, the doctor most certainly would have handed me a prescription for an antidepressant. But I didn't go to the clinic. I picked up this book, and something in my mood loosened: I felt miraculously *hopeful.* I handed five dollars to the vendor, took the book back to my bachelorette apartment and read it in one sitting.

It was the first book—the first *anything*—that challenged my concept of love and relationships, that opened my mind to what love might really mean, and in that, I found a measure of emotional relief. A way out. Picking the book up now, I find it hard to read all the way through. Its message is still powerful, but the text itself feels narrow and formulaic to me, maybe because I've learned so much more in the intervening years. I value it all the same because it made an impression that stuck.

Personal Power by Tony Robbins: People make fun of Tony Robbins—heck, people make fun self-help—but Tony Robbins taught me the power of momentum: one step in any direction will move you out of inertia, and into the next step and the next. It's a law of physics, actually, Newton's second law of motion. When you and Sarah were young, in the years before you went to school, I would listen to Tony on my cassette-playing Walkman (*archaic, I know*). We'd go for walks with the stroller, or to the playground, and I would have one ear tuned to Tony and one ear tuned to you. I was very stuck, as young mothers often are, with my whole world happily revolving around my young family, but my own separate identity seemingly evaporating.

One day I took a single step: I picked up the phone and called the local karate club. A month later we all went to a class, and that led to a few more steps. Three years and hundreds of hours of training after that, I had a black belt tied around my waist, a punching bag in the basement and a community of like-minded friends with wide-ranging backgrounds. And though I hung up my belt many years ago now, I know I can step back on the dojo floor or take a new fresh step in that direction any time.

Given the force of nature that you are, and your innate ability to take the initiative, this suggestion to *do something!* is not an idea that will be news to you. Still, on the off-chance that, say, you get concussed at a cheerleading practice and forget, or otherwise feel momentarily stuck, just remember the power of a single step. And if you're not inclined to reach for Tony Robbins, by all means remember Isaac Newton.

Turning the Mind into an Ally by Sakyong Mipham Rinpoche: I remember seeing this book propped up on the corner of a display in Chapters, the simple white cover with black and gold print, the title catching my attention. It was 2004, the same year I got my black-belt. *Turning the Mind into an Ally* was the first book I ever read about meditation and mindfulness, the first volume in what has become a huge collection of Buddhist books, books that survived all my cullings. The Sakyong is a marathon-running, horseback riding Tibetan-American monk. Rinpoche is a title of respect in Tibetan. It means precious one. Don't you love that? The precious Sakyong introduced me to the idea of working with my thoughts—which, by the way, are to be distinguished from *reality*—and showed me the impact that thoughts have on my emotional life, on how I see and interact with the world. This book likens the mind to a wild horse, one that needs to be tamed and trained lest it run off with us willy-nilly, which, if you stop and think about it, is exactly what happens. It is so obvious, isn't it? We train our physical muscles, so why don't we train our mental and emotional ones?

And so began my first few steps into *seeing* my escalating cycles of negative thinking. I realized how wild and unruly my thoughts were, how they would sometimes hijack my day, my life, turning it upside down. A thought like "Dad shouldn't leave his dishes and clothes and *stuff* laying about" might trail me quietly all week long, a slow-simmering anger stuffed under a guise of tolerance, an anger I wouldn't acknowledge until it erupted, usually in what would seem to be inexplicable circumstances: a single dish left on the counter for the one thousandth time. Those thoughts became the subject-matter of an experiment: *Hey, I'm caught in the middle of one of those thought-storms! What's going on here?* And that was the start of something new, of acknowledging and cooling down instead of boiling over.

Several titles by Pema Chödron: *Don't Bite the Hook Finding Freedom from Anger, Resentment and Other Destructive Emotions;*

Getting Unstuck: Breaking Your Habitual Patterns and Encountering Naked Reality; Living Beautifully with Uncertainty and Change; and so many more. Pema's name appears on the spines of more books in my collection than any other. What I love about her writing is the way she takes mindfulness concepts and Buddhist teachings and applies them to the most everyday of situations. And she doesn't hesitate to share her own hardest moments with humility and humour. She is a Buddhist nun. That sounds so cloistered and exotic, doesn't it? *A Buddhist nun. What have I got in common with a Buddhist nun?* Everything, as it turns out, by which I mean the ups and downs of ordinary life. Before Pema became a nun, she was an elementary school teacher and her name was Deirdre. Deirdre Blomfield-Brown. She was married, has two kids and lived in some nice American town. Then her husband came home and announced he was in love with someone else, and she threw a coffee mug at his head. From the brokenness of that moment she found a path out through Buddhism, through a life of meditation, mindfulness and working with her thoughts.

Pema isn't the only one who threw things. Once upon a time I heaved a pizza clear across the kitchen and then insisted you and Sarah clean it up. You two were about 6 and 8 year old at the time. Every so often you will remind me about it: "Yeah, Mom, remember the time you threw the pizza?" and we will shake our heads and laugh. *Silly Mom!* And then I will look up and see a faint oil stain on the ceiling over the sink, a stain made by chicken fried rice, also thrown in a moment of such profound frustration that it erupted in a Styrofoam box smashing against the kitchen wall. There were moments when I screamed at you until I was hoarse. Do you remember? Pema helped me see that there is another way out of those moments, that maybe the world isn't the way it appears—that maybe my _thoughts_ are the source of the trouble. She took me further down the road that the Sakyong had shown me and taught me that maybe, just maybe, there is a way through life that doesn't involve smashing pottery or throwing food.

Over the years I would upload Pema's audio books to my iPod and listen to them for hours while weeding the strawberry patch or rearranging the shrubs. She taught me how to sit still with the ugliest emotions and get to know them, to invite them in, instead of distracting myself or numbing out. You know what I mean: reaching for potato chips when you're not actually hungry or endlessly flipping television channels (not that we have television). Some folks reach for a cigarette or a rum and Coke, compulsive exercise or endless hours of work. Whatever it takes to stuff down an uncomfortable feeling, to distract us from feelings we don't want to feel.

Does sitting still with anger or fear sound like something to avoid? Does getting to know sadness or hurt sound uncomfortable? It _is_ uncomfortable, but once you find your way around it, it gets easier, and it is the way through and the way out. If the same pattern keeps repeating itself in your life, consider the possibility that it's your _thoughts_ and not the external circumstances that are the source of the problem, and that's good news because you can do something about it.

Your Inner Awakening and _Loving What Is_ by Byron Katie: Byron Katie's work is the practical counterpart to all my favourite

Buddhist teachers, offering a straightforward, step-by-step method to approach negative emotions and thoughts, a sort of crash-course in cognitive psychology. I refer back to Byron Katie anytime I find myself stuck in one of those spinning negative thought-storms. *Yeah, I see it, but how do I get out?* Byron Katie showed me how to see any stressful situation in a new light, to challenge what I think is true and to take responsibility for my thoughts and actions. Where my Buddhist teachers shone a light, Byron Katie gave me a toolkit. Do I think that so-and-so shouldn't have done such-and-such? Well, maybe that bears re-examining in a gentle, thoughtful way. Using her method, I can examine the relationship between thoughts and emotions, restore my focus and return a place where I can take practical, meaningful action.

An example: Dad shouldn't let his side of our shared office be such a mess. So? If I dwell on that thought, how do I feel? I feel lousy and powerless because I can't do anything about *his* being messy. And if I could drop that thought? If I could stop fussing myself about his being messy? How would I feel then? *Hmmm, let me sit quietly with that for a few minutes ... hey, I feel a whole lot freer if I'm not dwelling on that.* And hey, by the way, is there any place in your own life, Mom, where you're letting things be messy? *Oh, you mean like the kitchen counter? The van? Oh, and my messy thinking? Like maybe I'd be better off focussing on my own messes and not other people's? Right. Gotcha!* And not only that—are you *sure* Dad shouldn't be have a few messes around? I mean, do we really need two neatniks in the house? Isn't a little balance a good thing? *Yep, that is a good thing. I see your point.* And so it goes.

Byron Katie is like the Serenity Prayer brought to life: God, grant me the serenity to accept the things I cannot change, the courage to change the things I can and the wisdom to know the difference. If you ever feel stuck, Byron Katie can help you find a way out.

With *The Depression Cure* by Stephen Ilardi, don't be misled by the title. You don't need to be depressed, clinically or otherwise, to benefit from this book. It's just a good prescription for living: get sleep, move your body, step into the light, enjoy healthy social relationships, eat food (or supplements if necessary) that nourish your brain and have an anti-ruminating strategy. That last one refers to the very human habit of mentally chewing on an issue— "ruminating"—and the strategy is to consciously shifting your focus to a specific type of activity that will engage your attention. In other words, you have a escape hatch (just mind that your escape hatch doesn't become a permanent source of distraction). You have a good foundation in these habits already, but if you find yourself off-track, it can help to be reminded.

So when was this most helpful for me? In the winter of 2009 I was feeling so unreasonably blue that I finally went to our family doctor, young Dr. McNaull with the kind, blue eyes. I asked him to prescribe me an antidepressant. I felt *that* bad, and all my other strategies weren't working. "It's just a tool," he said, and I nodded. Then I went to the pharmacist, picked up the pills, brought them home and put them on the highest shelf in the kitchen. I never took them. Instead, I went online and searched *again* for some other way out. I found *The Depression Cure* and realized that as good as my mindfulness and cognitive strategies are, there was a whole range of other ways I needed to be taking care of myself. I'd forgotten. (And I forget, still, repeatedly, but nowadays I get back on track a lot faster.)

And maybe this isn't the place to launch into it, but I think some degree of depression—or melancholy, as they called it in the old days, or "the black dog" in the words of Winston Churchill—is part of the human experience. We've talked about this. Most importantly, if you find yourself feeling low, blue, sad or lonely for an extended period of time, do something about it. Don't do what I did. Don't put a mask on that says, "I'm fine, really, I'm okay." *I'm tough. I'm strong. Stiff upper lip and all that.*

Bull feathers.

I did that for *years* because I didn't know better. You can benefit from my having not known and reach out instead, reach for the boosters and additives I've listed here and others you will find on your own.

As for books, there are many other well-thumbed and highlighted volumes on my shelf. The ones listed here are a handful of those that have had the most impact, that have proven the most effective at loosening stains, softening the wash water of daily life and, yes, preventing the redeposit of soil.

I know you will build your own sacred stack of books, find your own laundry aids and boosters and that yours will look different from mine, just as your path through life is uniquely your own. You'll have your own inspirations, triumphs and struggles, and you'll find your own way through the laundry pile of life.

Chapter 15

DIPPY EGGS BY GRAMPER

Set table for breakfast.

Place eggs in sauce pan. Cover completely with water.

Set burner to high. Watch pot until water boils. (Apparently there is a saying about this.)

Once the water has achieved a rollicking boil, turn heat down to maintain a consistent simmer.

Set your time for three minutes. Also, it is better not to leave the kitchen, lest you get distracted and end up with rock-hard eggs suitable for use only as projectiles.

Start toast.

When time is up, gently rescue the eggs from the pot using a slotted spoon and deposit in waiting bowl of cool water. This stops the cooking process. Butter the toast and cut it into fingers.

Place into egg cups. Admire your handiwork, and enjoy! PS: yes, I realize you already know how to make these.

What to Do if You Spill the Dippy Part on Your Shirt

Gently scrape off any crusted bits. Dad would suggest eating if off with your teeth, but I don't recommend that approach because of the risk of fabric damage. Besides, it's rather *uncouth*, as Juney might say.

Soak in cold water with a bit of laundry detergent and colour-safe bleach (like OxiClean, a 1:2 proportion of dish soap and peroxide).

Wash as usual. If the stain persists after washing, repeat the process above. It may take multiple treatments.

If the garment is dry-clean only, all you can really do is head to the dryer cleaner and point.

Chapter 16

THE FINAL RINSE

A Postscript —On Advice Not Followed and the Way Life Unfolds

I learned a lot in the course of writing this book, not only about laundry but about the nature of writing and life. Words, it turns out, need time to rest on the page, rather like stains soaking. If you let them sit overnight, you can pick them up the next day and see them with fresh eyes.

Also, both laundry and writing benefit from good light.

And despite all the gathered wisdom here, let me confess that I don't always follow it myself.

I still don't load the washing machine in the technically correct fashion. As far as I can tell, the clothes aren't any the worse for it.

I don't *always* shake out the clothes between the washer and the dryer either (unless there's been a tissue incident).

And in the end, I didn't install the outdoor clothesline. After fully six weeks of having the unopened box in our garage, I returned it to the store.

Why?

Because the indoor clotheslines I have are good enough. For now.

The indoor clotheslines are located *precisely* where I am removing the laundry from the washing machine and dryer. This is a great setup. It might even be perfect. Using an outdoor line meant opening and closing two doors on the way outside, probably tripping over shopping bins and sports equipment along the way, plus a set of stairs to navigate, all while carrying a basket of laundry in my hands. Visions of tumbling down the stairs began to dance in my head, along with clean laundry and me landing in the mud.

Then there would be the seasonal routine. We'd need to put the clothesline up in the springtime and away again in the fall, carefully packing it and storing it in the garage. Have you seen how much stuff is in there already? We might actually lose it amid the bocce balls and the bins of old Barbie dolls.

And what about the weather? In the summer of your graduation year, we were lucky to see three hours of sunshine before the clouds moved in and the rain started. Opportunities for hanging clothes on a line outdoors were precious few. And then winter comes.

Still, I'm glad I did the research. Next summer I may change my mind again, put up that clothesline and write about the experience. Perhaps the robins and sparrows in the neighbourhood would appreciate the gesture.

In any case, life goes like this. We undertake our research, form opinions and lay out plans … and then we might just as quickly dispense with it all, realizing that maybe, just maybe, *easy* is important too and that *pretty good* is good enough.

In the end, it all comes out in the wash.

Resources

FOR LAUNDRY AND LIFE

Audiobooks

Chödron, P (2007). *Don't Bite the Hook Finding Freedom from Anger, Resentment and Other Destructive Emotions,* Boulder, CO: Shambhala Audio. Catch habitual patterns as they unfold and find a better way. Just noticing that you've been triggered—even if it's too late to stop the reaction—can help you find a more compassionate way through life.

Chödron, P (2007).*Getting Unstuck: Breaking Your Habitual Patterns and Encountering Naked Reality,* Louisville, CO: Sounds True. Learn to identify and sit with that "hooked feeling" — called *shenpa* in Tibetan—rather than reacting.

Katie, B. (2003). *Your Inner Awakening: The Work of Byron Katie: Four questions that will transform your life,* New York: Three Rivers Press. Never mind the New-Age-ish sounding title: if you want to understand how to disentangle yourself from useless cycles of thought, this is a must-listen—and check out the videos of the Work online, too. Kind of wish she wouldn't capitalize *Work,* but hey, *Whatever.*

Robbins, T (1996). *Personal Power*, Santa Monica: Guthy-Renker. Robbins is a master at motivation. My reading is more nuanced now, but I'll forever be grateful for his helping me realize that I could *do something* at a time when I was so exhausted that I didn't see how it was possible. A classic of the nineties self-help genre.

Books

Chödron, P (2003, 2006). *Always Maintain a Joyful Mind and Other Lojong Teachings on Awakening Compassion and Fearlessness*, (Boston): Shambhala. This book contains a list of Buddhist slogans that provide guidance for everyday living. Among my favourites: *Don't expect applause* and *be grateful to everyone*.

Chödron, P (2012). *Living Beautifully with Uncertainty and Change*, (Boston): Shambhala. This book — one of the fifteen or so Chödron volumes on my shelf—teaches on the "Three Commitments: not causing harm, taking care of each other and embracing the world just as it is. A life's work in three not-so-easy steps.

Jampolsky, G (1970). *Love Is Letting Go of Fear*, (New York): Bantam Books. This book defines love by distinguishing it from fear. Once this idea takes hold in your mind—and heart— the world will never look the same again.

Katie, B. (2003). *Loving What Is Four questions that can change your life*, New York: Three Rivers Press. Hands down the best practical how-to guide for freeing yourself from damaging negative thinking.

Mendelson, C (2005). *Home Comforts: The Art and Science of Keeping House*, New York: Scribner. This book is a housekeeping encyclopaedia covering laundry, as well as every other aspect of home management, in excruciating detail. A necessity! At 886 pages, it also makes an excellent door stop.

Sakyong Mipham Rinpoche (2004). *Turning the Mind into an Ally*, New York: Riverhead Books. The Sakyong teaches us that the mind is like a wild horse. Learning to tame and train our minds helps us live with kindness, compassion and equanimity.

Zukowksi, S (2009). *Salt, Lemons, Vinegar and Baking Soda*, London: Metro Books. This book covers household cleaning in general, but the laundry tips alone are worth the price. I've saved a few much-loved white blouses and T-shirts using lemon juice and vinegar. Who knew?

Online Resources

There are thousands of online articles, blogs, videos and pins (via Pinterest) about laundry. These are a few of my favourites:

http://www.davidsuzuki.org/: David Suzuki's website has a mountain of great information and ideas for cleaning without chemicals as well as living green in general. For instance:

Is there formaldehyde in no-iron shirts? at http://www.davidsuzuki.org/what-you-can-do/queen-of-green/faqs/cleaning/is-there-formaldehyde-in-no-iron-shirts/

Stain Removal, David Suzuki's Queen of Green (three-page online article) http://www.davidsuzuki.org/publications/qog-stainremoval.pdf (See also QueenofGreen.ca.)

Real Simple magazine, *Laundry Tips* section: http://www.realsimple.com/home-organizing/cleaning/laundry/laundry-tips-00000000055555. Offers a wide range of practical articles on laundry management.

If you want to get fancy and complicated, you can also check out Martha Stewart online.

Care Labels

For information about care labelling, check out

A Guide to United States Apparel and Household Textiles Compliance Requirements, published by the National Institute of Standards and Technology, US Department of Commerce: http://gsi.nist.gov/global/docs/apparel_guide.pdf.

Guide to the Textile Labelling and Advertising Regulations, Competition Bureau: http://www.competitionbureau.gc.ca/eic/site/cb-bc.nsf/eng/01249.html.

US standards are much more rigorous and detailed than their Canadian counterparts.

For a handy chart of the various label symbols, see "Laundry Guide to Common Care Symbols," http://www.textileaffairs.com/lguide.htm. Or just Google it.